Moments With God

The Complete Collection of Rosary Meditations

Patti J. Smith

~~~~~~~

Included as Part of the Collection

AND GOD STILL LOVES ME
A Journey from the Dark Abyss of Sin to God's Mercy

First Edition

Published by
Helping Hands Press

ISBN: 978-1-62208-524-8

Printed in the United States of America

Contents

A Mended Heart
Rosary Meditations on Forgiveness

A Mended Heart focuses on forgiveness of family, friends, attitudes and those lost in a world of perversion and crime and addresses those offenses that we have buried deep within our souls; secrets we have protected for years. This devotional offers a way to open up our hearts and ask for God's mercy on our offenders, which in turn will lighten our life and remove the roadblocks on our journey.

Journey To Sunset
Rosary Meditations for Caregivers

When someone we love becomes dependent due to advanced age, illness or injury, we are faced with a difficult decision ... a nursing home absent familiar surroundings or in-home care by a stranger. After a great deal of soul-searching, a third option is chosen ... we do it ourselves. The responsibility is enormous and the challenges daunting. Our life becomes an emotional roller coaster. Hope will dwindle and faith will falter if we do not turn to OUR care-giver, the Divine Caregiver ... God.

Redeemed
Rosary Meditations for Post-Abortive Women

An unplanned pregnancy can be a joyous occasion but for some women a frightening one. A young girl does not want to face her parents, an unmarried woman is worried about her career, a mother with many other children lives in poverty. Succumbing to fear or pressure from friends and family results in the decision to abort. At first there is a sense of relief; however, a few months, years, or decades later the effects of that decision may surface with disastrous results. The physical effects can be dealt with medically; however, it takes the unfathomable mercy of God to heal the soul.

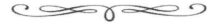

Embrace The Morning
Rosary Meditations to Calm The Storm

Our lives are in continual flux and with the stresses of life, we succumb to the pressure ... forgetting to set aside time for God. By doing this, we become engulfed in a maelstrom. This devotional presents meditations and prayers that will speak to our daily struggles. We need to remember, God is our safe harbor. Cultivating a deep-rooted relationship with Him is essential if we are to weather the storm.

How to Pray the Rosary

And God Still Loves Me
A Journey From the Dark Abyss of Sin to God's Mercy

We all at times wish we could turn back the hands of time and have a "do-over", and I was desperate for one. I wanted to forget and erase the pain inflicted on my family, friends and myself. Most of all I wanted to die. This book is about a lost soul who shunned God and hurt everyone in her path. It's about a sinner who has fallen short but through God's love, grace and mercy has come around to know God's glory.

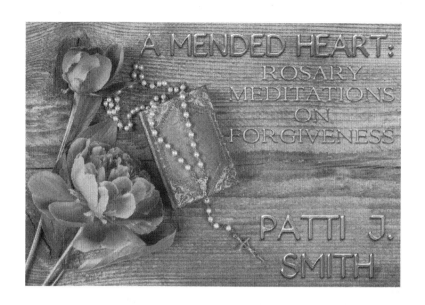

Take away the chains of hate
that fill my world with strife.
They come from past resentments
I've held throughout my life.

Dear Jesus, open up my heart
to forgive and be set free.
May I be as merciful
as you have been towards me.

Introduction

Matthew 18:21-22: Then Peter came up and said to him, "Lord, how often shall my brother sin against me, and I forgive him? As many as seven times?" Jesus said to him, "I do not say to you seven times, but seventy times seven."

Forgiveness is one of the greatest gifts we can give to a person, but it is also the most difficult. My life has been peppered with events that can only be described as excruciating and humiliating; some self-inflicted and some through no fault of my own. Regardless of how the events originated, they weighed heavily on my heart. It wasn't until I attended Rachel's Hope, a healing retreat for post-abortive women, I realized the importance of forgiveness in my faith journey. We have all been hurt by others, witnessed hurt or caused it ourselves. If we are not open to forgiveness, these hurts will fester and imprison us in a world of hopelessness, grief, resentment and anger which, in turn, distances us from God.

When we forgive, we are emulating what Jesus did on the cross. Regardless what was done to us or others, it is nothing compared to what Jesus experienced, and that is what we need to remember each and every day.

These meditations are a way to reflect on the gift of forgiveness. They will give us the ability to heal our heart and soul and bring us closer to God and His will for us.

The Joyful Mysteries
Forgiving Family

I. The Annunciation

Behold, I am the handmaid of the Lord; let it be to me according to your word. (Luke 1:38)

Our Blessed Mother Mary, at first was frightened and apprehensive when the angel Gabriel told her of God's plan. However, because her faith was strong and she trusted God implicitly, she opened her heart, mind and soul to His will.

The unconditional trust Blessed Mother demonstrated is much like the trust instilled in us when we are born. It is absolutely natural to trust that our families will love and care for us.

Unfortunately, this trust is sometimes violated. Promises are broken; we are used as pawns in shattered marriages; treated as servants and property; shuffled from relative to relative, given no stability; assigned too much responsibility at a young age and robbed of our childhood.

Dear Jesus, no one is perfect except you and our Blessed Mother. Help me see that no matter how the trust was violated; those actions were not of God but of human imperfection. Guide me to understand those actions may not have been intentional, but part of a pattern that existed long before I was born. Provide me with the necessary wisdom, knowledge and humility to identify those patterns in my own life and show me how to prevent them from continuing.

My Lord, please be merciful to my offenders, to me if I have offended, and open my heart to forgiveness.

II. The Visitation

In those days Mary arose and went with haste into the hill country, to a town in Judah, and she entered the house of Zechariah and greeted Elizabeth. (Luke 1:39-40)

Even though Mary was pregnant, she put aside her own discomfort and traveled a great distance to help Elizabeth.

Family members sometimes fall short in helping us or giving us encouragement we need to succeed in life. We are told our dreams and goals are foolish and cannot be accomplished; we are punished or laughed at for failing instead of rewarded and praised for success; we are compared to other siblings; we are not loved equally.

Jesus, our emotional needs at times were not met. We lived in fear of failure and diminished self-esteem. Instead of reaching for the stars, we eluded our dreams and lowered our expectations. Our lack of self-confidence and avoidance of challenges resulted in many lost opportunities. We became resentful towards our family for creating such a weakling and for not encouraging us to succeed.

Help me, dear Jesus, to see my worth and free me from my insecurities. Provide me the capacity to be supportive and impartial; to encourage the acceptance of challenges; inspire dreams; to reward success and console failure.

Please be merciful to my offenders, to me if I have offended, and open my heart to forgiveness.

III. The Nativity

Be not afraid; for behold, I bring you good news of a great joy which will come to all the people; for to you is born this day in the city of David a Savior, who is Christ the Lord. (Luke 2:10-11)

God gave us a savior at Bethlehem and that child was brought into this world with joyous anticipation and love.

All children should be as welcomed as Jesus, but sadly it is not always the case. Some of us were told from the very beginning we were a "mistake" or "an accident". When we enter the world unexpectedly, our parent(s) may be overwhelmed and lash out. The blame is centered on us for their predicaments. We may have caused them to drop out of school; because of us there is financial instability, lack of employment opportunities and loss of freedom; if it weren't for us there wouldn't have been a dysfunctional marriage.

Carrying this burden as a child is devastating. We heard those words so many times we began to believe we were mistakes and truly felt our existence was a hindrance. We grow up trapped in a world of guilt and self-hatred.

Jesus, please send the light of joy into expectant mothers **and** fathers. Have them realize a child is a blessing from You and was part of Your plan.

Please be merciful to my offenders, to me if I have offended, and open my heart to forgiveness.

IV. The Presentation

When Joseph and Mary had done everything required by the Law of the Lord, they returned to Galilee to their own town of Nazareth. And the child grew and became strong; he was filled with wisdom, and the grace of God was on him. (Luke 2:39-40)

Mary and Joseph presented Jesus to the temple as prescribed by Jewish law. Their faith was the foundation for everything in their lives and they imparted that to Jesus by word and action.

Sadly, in this day and age, the foundation of faith is cracking. Faith is no longer the cornerstone of the family. We are raised focused on earthly rewards rather than spiritual ones. Career advancement, money, large homes, nice cars and expensive vacations are the ultimate priorities. Being active in a faith community, volunteering and sacrificing time for the less fortunate is considered extravagant or inconvenient. It is also considered old-fashioned and not gratifying. This path of self-centeredness and selfishness is filled with trappings that open the door for Satan and his minions to lead us astray.

Jesus, help me focus more on faith in my family and show me the way to bring others back to You.

Please be merciful to my offenders, to me if I have offended, and open my heart to forgiveness.

V. The Finding of Jesus in the Temple

And when they saw him they were astonished; and his mother said to him, "Son, why have you treated us so? Behold, your father and I have been looking for you anxiously. (Luke 2:48)

When Jesus was lost in the temple, Mary and Joseph were understandably distraught. All they could think about was their son's safety and welfare.

Many of us were abandoned and neglected by parents who selfishly put their own desires first or were not capable of taking on the responsibility of a child. We were raised in homes with parents that were just children themselves or homes fueled with alcohol, drugs and other excesses. We were supervised by video games, locked doors, and strangers or just left to our own devices. There was always the nightmare of no one coming home, the door would remain locked, or the strangers would leave as well. That terrifying nightmare triggered such insecurity we became untrusting, timid, and overly protective of our feelings. We sabotaged any relationship that threatened to be more intimate.

Jesus, heal me from the pain of abandonment and the fear of intimacy. Give me the courage to trust and be open to love.

Please be merciful to my offenders, to me if I have offended, and open my heart to forgiveness.

The Luminous Mysteries
Forgiving Those with Damaging Attitudes and Lifestyles

I. The Baptism in the Jordan

Then Jesus came from Galilee to the Jordan to John, to be baptized by him. John would have prevented him, saying, "I need to be baptized by you, and do you come to me?" But Jesus answered him, "Let it be so now; for thus it is fitting for us to fulfill all righteousness." (Matthew 3:13-15)

Baptism is a new beginning, becoming a child of God. It represents love and acceptance.

In our day to day lives we have come across people, familiar or strangers, that belittle us because we are different. We may have a different skin color, come from another culture,be overweight, scarred, handicapped or mentally challenged. People treat these differences as imperfections, dirty, frightening, or evil. They walk by us with sneers, point at us and laugh, or they go out of their way to avoid any type of contact whatsoever. There are also those who pity and patronize us. They do everything for us, even if we are capable because they assume we are not. If we resist help we are ungrateful and if we accept, we are taking advantage. We become ashamed of who we are and shy away from people, places and activities. We feel unwelcomed, ugly and unloved.

Jesus, please guide me to be more compassionate, loving, tolerant, and accepting towards those different than me and help me be an example for others.

Please be merciful to my offenders, to me if I have offended, and open my heart to forgiveness.

II. The Wedding at Cana

On the third day there was a marriage at Cana in Galilee, and the mother of Jesus was there; [2] Jesus also was invited to the marriage, with his disciples. (John 2:1-2)

Jesus' disciples wanted to be close to Him; they wanted to know Him and learn from Him. They knew the only way to happiness and fulfillment was through Him.

Unfortunately, there are those in our lives that are lacking those desires. They tempt us with promises of happiness and fulfillment through perversion. We are inundated with media that promotes promiscuity, alcohol and drug abuse, violence and other self-destructive behavior. Instead of being warned against this type of behavior, we are thrust into it by our peers and by others who will benefit financially. We are led to believe this is the only way to be accepted in society and that failure to follow will result in being labeled an outcast. Although we know the difference between right and wrong, we are sometimes torn between the two for fear of rejection or being excluded.

Jesus, please strengthen my defenses against temptations and give me the courage to remain faithful to You and Your teachings.

Please be merciful to my offenders, to me if I have offended, and open my heart to forgiveness.

III. The Proclamation of the Kingdom

As he landed he saw a great throng, and he had compassion on them, because they were like sheep without a shepherd; and he began to teach them many things. (Mark 6:34)

God sent Jesus to proclaim His Kingdom. To do this Jesus devoted himself to teaching God's word and giving hope to the world.

We too are called to share His glory and teach His word. We are called to be <u>like</u> Jesus. This calling is sometimes ridiculed by non-believers. Their hearts and minds are closed to the reality there is a creator of Heaven and Earth, a Savior who died for our sins or accept there is life everlasting. Disappointingly, there are those who succumb to the ridicule, forsake their faith then try to persuade others to follow.

My Dear Lord, how frightening life would be without you. Protect me from the influence of non-believers and give me the words to gently guide them towards You. Give me the courage to continue spreading the Word and stand firm on my beliefs. Help me show them the blessings you bestow upon us each and every day and all the beauty in this world You created. Through me, Lord, speak to them and give them hope and peace.

Please be merciful to my offenders, to me if I have offended, and open my heart to forgiveness.

IV. The Transfiguration

And a cloud overshadowed them, and a voice came out of the cloud, "This is my beloved Son; listen to him." (Mark 7)

During the transfiguration, Peter, James and John saw Jesus as human and divine. God announced to them Jesus was his Son and to listen to him. We are bound to the same edict as Peter, James and John … to listen.

Dearest Jesus, we are surrounded by people with deviant lifestyles who proclaim their ways do not go against Your teachings. They manipulate Your words of love; forgiveness and acceptance in order to justify their immorality. We are expected to accept their interpretation of Your word and disregard everything we had ever been taught. We are expected to consider their behavior as normal and are expected to allow our children to be taught the same.

Please keep my ears and eyes open to hear and see the truth. Do not allow me to blindly accept the unacceptable. Through love and tolerance, help me guide the misguided. Help me explain to them Your words do not condone deviancy, but offer love, forgiveness and acceptance upon repentance. Help me walk with them on the path of redemption.

Please be merciful to my offenders, to me if I have offended, and open my heart to forgiveness.

V. The Institution of the Eucharist

And as they were eating, he took bread, and blessed, and broke it, and gave it to them, and said, "Take; this is my body." And he took a cup, and when he had given thanks he gave it to them, and they all drank of it. (Mark 14:22-24)

The Eucharist is the body and blood of Jesus which provides nourishment for our souls and unites us all at His table of life.

The culture of death exists in our world. Supporters of this culture are starved and separated from the banquet and will ultimately extinguish the light of life if not challenged and saved.

Millions of babies are aborted every year and the mothers are encouraged or coerced to do so. Unplanned pregnancies are considered inconvenient to a career, young women are afraid of telling their parents, an unmarried woman is embarrassed, the baby might have medical issues, or an abortion is used as a form of birth control. There is no discouragement of abortion; it's considered a "routine" procedure. We are led to believe it is not a child but just tissue and told there will be no ill effects. Nothing is further from the truth. Abortion takes the lives of innocents and also takes an emotional and physical toll on the mothers and fathers, which can lead to drastic consequences.

Many inmates each year are being put to death to atone for crimes they committed. It is important that society is protected, and it is by keeping criminals behind high walls, razor fences and bars. Regardless what types of crimes are committed, Jesus is always open to repentance and everyone deserves that chance. Taking away that opportunity by execution goes against all of His teachings.

Jesus, please show me how I can challenge this culture of death and save those involved. Life is so very precious, at conception all the way through natural death.

Please be merciful to my offenders, to me if I have offended, and open my heart to forgiveness.

The Sorrowful Mysteries
Forgiveness of Friends
and Acquaintances

I. Agony in the Garden

Then he came to the disciples and said to them, "Are you still sleeping and taking your rest? Behold, the hour is at hand, and the Son of man is betrayed into the hands of sinners. Rise, let us be going; see, my betrayer is at hand." (Matthew 26:45-46)

Christ was alone in that garden. He had asked if at least one of his disciples would sit with him, but his pleas were not heard.

We too are at times left alone, estranged and forgotten. Our cries for help go unnoticed. When we are sad, mourning or frightened, all we need is a sympathetic ear, someone to tell us they understand or just give us a warm, loving embrace. To suffer alone and in silence is excruciating and worsens the grief and fear.

Jesus, I know the pain of suffering alone and in silence. I longed for words of understanding and comforting arms around me; for someone to share my tears. Help me hear the cries of help from my friends. May I show them compassion, understanding and warmth in their time of need. May I shed tears with them and lovingly support them as a true friend should.

Please be merciful to my offenders, to me if I have offended, and open my heart to forgiveness.

II. The Scourging at the Pillar

Then Pilate took Jesus and scourged him. (John 19:1)

Christ suffered immeasurable pain as he was scourged. He could have stopped it; however, he bravely allowed it to continue as it was His sacrifice for us.

Some relationships can cause a great deal of pain, emotionally and physically, yet we allow them to continue, but for the wrong reasons. We continue because we know of no other way, we are afraid of retribution, or afraid of being alone. We continue because we believe in the vows we took or the commitment we made. We continue because we don't want to break up a family. And at times continue, sadly enough, because we convince ourselves we deserve what we are getting.

We have suffered physical and emotional bruises that are used to keep us compliant and dependent. We have been intimidated and demoralized to the point we believe we cannot function in the world on our own. We want to believe the apologies and acts of contrition, just to see the monster rear its ugly head again and again.

Jesus, please help me see the difference between true sacrifice and fear. Give me the courage to try and heal relationships but also give me the strength to walk away if necessary.

Please be merciful to my offenders, to me if I have offended, and open my heart to forgiveness.

III.   The Crowning with Thorns

And the soldiers plaited a crown of thorns, and put it on his head, and arrayed him in a purple robe (John 19:2)

Christ suffered humiliation when that crown of thorns was thrust upon his head. Certain people in our lives humiliate us in a variety of ways such as admonishing us in front of others, teasing, talking behind our backs, lying about us and not acknowledging our worth. We are faced with these circumstances throughout our lives and try to remain positive and ignore it; however, it is so difficult to do.

Demoralizing, false and spiteful words echo in our minds. Although we know the truth, the doubt grows. We understand that demeaning others is a way a person deals with his or her own insecurities or perceived inadequacies, but subconsciously we try to find fault within ourselves. For some reason, if it is our fault the pain won't be as excruciating.

Jesus, help me refrain from words and actions that humiliate by reminding me of the pain I experienced. Give me the courage to face those who have caused me pain, and with compassion and kindness, reveal to them the consequences of their actions.

Be merciful to my offenders, to me if I have offended, and open my heart to forgiveness.

IV.   The Carrying of the Cross

And as they led him away, they seized one Simon of Cyre'ne, who was coming in from the country, and laid on him the cross, to carry it behind Jesus. (Luke 23:26)

When Christ carried his cross and fell, Simon of Cyre'ne was ordered to help Him. He balked and resisted.

Unfortunately, the same is true today. Helping another person is considered a weakness ... a "what's in it for me" proposition. If there is no benefit, there is no help. Many are felled with poverty, homelessness and despair. There are those who perceive the falling as self-inflicted, therefore, not deserving of help. The unfortunates do not ask to be destitute; they do not take delight living under bridges, with dirty clothes; they don't take pleasure in being cold and hungry. They are in these situations for a variety of reasons ... job loss, divorce, illness, addiction. They have abilities and skills and would like nothing more than to pick themselves up and start a new life.

Jesus, when I am given a cross in my life that is Your will, help me to not be angry and resentful. Help me embrace my cross as you embraced yours. Give me the strength not to run away from it but to carry it with resignation and unite my suffering with yours. When others are in trouble, help me share in the carrying of their crosses. Help me to see that we are all one step away from those less fortunate.

Please be merciful to my offenders, to me if I have offended, and open my heart to forgiveness.

V. The Crucifixion

And Jesus said, "Father, forgive them; for they know not what they do." (Luke 23:34)

During the crucifixion, Jesus held no animosity towards his torturers. He was bloodied, hanging from the cross and in indescribable pain and still, with great love and compassion, forgave them.

Admitting fault is difficult enough but asking for forgiveness is one of the most difficult and humbling experiences we can face. Pride and embarrassment sometimes holds us back but we know it is absolutely necessary to admit our faults and make amends. We become vulnerable in our humility and repentance; we are sincere and anticipate forgiveness.

Unfortunately, there are some who refuse to forgive. The past is continually recalled and we are constantly rebuked. Carrying grudges instead of forgiving inhibits the ability to be truly happy and creates a detachment from God and His will. Whatever the transgression, there is nothing that cannot be forgiven. Jesus sets the ultimate example.

Jesus, help me to forgive, let go and move forward. Do not allow my anger and disappointments to fester and distance me from You. Have my willingness to forgive set an example for others.

Please be merciful to my offenders, to me if I have offended, and open my heart to forgiveness.

The Glorious Mysteries
Forgiveness of Those Who Do Evil

I. The Resurrection

And he said to them, "Do not be amazed; you seek Jesus of Nazareth, who was crucified. He has risen, he is not here…" (Mark 16:6)

The resurrection shows us that Jesus triumphed over death and evil.

Many in our society are evil and have committed unspeakable crimes. The motives are varied; however, none are justified. Questions abound as to what would trigger someone to take another's life but the fact remains, a person died and it was by another's hand. There is so much anger and hate in our hearts when someone we love is taken from us under these circumstances. We want revenge, we want the perpetrator to hurt and suffer like our loved one. Our hearts are so broken, forgiveness is not even considered.

The grief will pass eventually; however, the anger and hate remains. As with any other transgression against us, we cannot be freed from the anger and hate until we forgive. We are not just holding back our happiness; we are clouding the wonderful memories of our lost loved one. Instead of remembering and celebrating the beauty of that life, we are obsessing on what caused the death.

Jesus, please let the sun shine through on the life of our lost loved ones; remembering the joy and love we shared. Give us the words to pray the guilty be triumphant over evil.

Please be merciful to my offenders, to me if I have offended, and open my heart to forgiveness.

II. The Ascension

But you shalt receive power when the Holy Spirit has come upon you; and you shalt be my witnesses in Jerusalem and in all Judea and Samaria and to the end of the earth. (Acts 1:8)

Prior to His ascension, Jesus told his disciples they will receive the light of the Holy Spirit and will spread His word to the world until the end of time. Those living in darkness of evil do not see the light, as it is shrouded by Satan. They do not know how to escape. They are encouraged to prey on us and engulf us in terror, in an attempt to force us into a life filled with fear and trepidation.

So many lives have been taken by so-called martyrs who believe their acts of terror and sacrifice of their own lives will bring rewards in the afterlife. They proclaim they are following their faith; however, that faith was contorted to justify evil. We look at them with hate, anger and fear instead of with pity. Their souls have been deceived by Satan's lies and can only be reclaimed through our forgiveness and prayers.

Jesus, please pull away Satan's shroud and shine the light of love into their souls.

Please be merciful to my offenders, to me if I have offended and open my heart to forgiveness.

III.   The Descent of the Holy Spirit

And there appeared to them tongues as of fire, distributed and resting on each one of them. And they were all filled with the Holy Spirit and began to speak in other tongues, as the Spirit gave them utterance. (Acts 2:3-4)

The Holy Spirit will descend upon all of us and lighten our lives if we open our hearts and souls.

In our daily lives we are continually faced with temptation. There are predators ... drug dealers, prostitutes, pornographers, etc. on the streets looking to exploit the weak.   These predators have only one goal ... to ensnare us into their dark existence and bring more along.   We are promised material riches, a good time, acceptance and love; things we all desire. By the time we realize the lies, it's too late. We are broken, dependent, morally and physically bankrupt.

These predators know no other way. They believe the lies and are as broken as their victims. Their hearts have been locked tight and jailed by the bars of Satan.

Jesus, remove the bars, unlock their hearts and replace the darkness with light of the Holy Spirit.

Please be merciful to my offenders, to me if I have offended, and open my heart to forgiveness.

IV.   The Assumption of Mary

In the sixth month the angel Gabriel was sent from God to a city of Galilee named Nazareth, to a virgin betrothed to a man whose name was Joseph, of the house of David; and the virgin's name was Mary. (Luke 1:26-17)

Mary was assumed, body and soul, into heaven because of her purity. That purity was protected and held in reverence throughout her life on earth as well as in heaven.

Purity and innocence should always be protected and held in reverence; however, they are both being savagely stolen from us by ungodly desires. The savagery leaves us feeling unworthy of love, even from God. Our lives are stained with shame. We hate the perpetrator but we blame ourselves for allowing it to happen. We try to forget. The memories haunt us in our dreams and prevent us from growing emotionally and spiritually. We protect our secret by any means possible. We fear if the secret is discovered we would be detested and scorned. We are certain God knows what happened and has already deserted us.

Jesus, wrap your comforting and loving arms around all of us who feel unworthy and deserted. Wash away the stain of shame and open our hearts and souls to see You were always there and would never abandon us. Jesus, wrap your healing arms around the wicked and free them from their ungodly desires.

Please be merciful to my offenders, to me if I have offended, and open my heart to forgiveness.

V. The Coronation of Mary

A great sign appeared in the sky, a woman clothed with the sun, with the moon under her feet and on her head a crown of twelve stars. (Revelation 12:1)

Mary was made Queen of Heaven and mother to us all. Her love is endless and unconditional.

As much as Mary loves, there are those in our world filled with that much envy and greed. It permeates their minds and souls which ultimately perpetuates evil. It lives in those who steal, corrupt, misrepresent, and mislead. There is no remorse, regret or concern for consequences. There is no apprehension. Everything is justified, and unfortunately socially acceptable. The envious and greedy strive for material things, money, prestige, advancement and control through whatever means possible. A person has value only by who they are, what they have and how they can be used.

When we fall prey, we feel the same emotions as if we were physically victimized: fear, guilt, shame, worthlessness. Jesus, please shine down on those filled with envy and greed and change their hearts. Help us show them Your way leads to the real reward.

Please be merciful to my offenders, to me if I have offended, and open my heart to forgiveness.

A Note From The Author

When meditating on forgiveness we should feel released from a very heavy burden. The tears that flow will cleanse and refresh the soul. I firmly believe God holds us in his arms when we open up old wounds, and new ones, to forgiveness. Through the Holy Spirit He sends us the courage and strength to finally heal.

It is important too, that during these meditations, to include ourselves. I know through experience that forgiving myself was a task I was not willing to undertake for quite some time. To acknowledge my faults was one thing, but to forgive them was a different story altogether. I was convinced the consequences I suffered were deserved and the shame was something I would have to live with forever as penance.

A final thought … when we acknowledge our sins and repent to Him, He forgives us. Who are we to think we can undo what He has already done? So praise Him, thank Him, and move forward with a renewed heart and spirit.

MOM

There doesn't seem to be much time to tell you everything,
your mind is slipping way too fast.
I tell you how much you mean to me,
but the words don't seem to last.

I want you to look back and smile on all our family times.
but now there's just blank stares.
I try to remind you with photos,
but the memories just aren't there.

Where are you mom, you've gone somewhere,
a place where I can't go.
Help me get to where you are,
because I miss you so.

Book Cover: Copy of an original oil painting of my parents, entitled "My Neighbors". Beautifully created by Alexsandra (Sasha) Babic, MFA, Vista, CA

Introduction

2 Corinthians 1:3-7: "Blessed be the God and Father of our Lord Jesus Christ, the Father of compassion and God of all encouragement, who encourages us in our every affliction, so that we may be able to encourage those who are in any affliction with the encouragement with which we ourselves are encouraged by God. For as Christ's sufferings overflow to us, so through Christ does our encouragement also overflow. If we are afflicted, it is for your encouragement and salvation; if we are encouraged, it is for your encouragement, which enables you to endure the same sufferings that we suffer. Our hope for you is firm, for we know that as you share in the sufferings, you also share in the encouragement."

One minute we are happy and carefree, knowing all is right in our world. We set our goals and mapped our course. Then life takes a detour...an illness or accident befalls a parent, spouse or other family member which results in their loss of independence and need for continued care. We are aware there are professionals that could take care of our loved ones; however, we balk at the thought of having them in unfamiliar surroundings or having strangers in their home. We pray for guidance and the answer comes directly from our hearts.

This devotional is for the caregiver on a journey that can be filled with pain, sadness, fear and anger. But through God's abundant compassion, can also be filled with happiness, hope and peace.

The Joyful Mysteries

I. The Annunciation

Luke 1:36-37: And behold, Elizabeth, your relative, has also conceived a son in her old age, and this is the sixth month for her who was called barren; for nothing will be impossible for God.

As Elizabeth discovers she is with child at such an advanced age, one can only imagine her reaction. She would, of course, be filled with wonder; however, also enter into a state of disbelief. This state is also experienced when faced with the incapacity or mortality of a loved one. We put up barriers in our mind to prevent the reality from filtering in. We put on a "happy mask", and continue on with life as if nothing is wrong – at least for awhile.

Jesus, I was not prepared for the challenge set before me and need Your help. Free me from denial so I can focus on my loved one. Provide me with the strength to move forward with love, compassion and determination.

My Loving Savior, Divine Caregiver, walk with me through this journey and always.

II. The Visitation

Luke 1:39-40: During those days Mary set out and traveled to the hill country in haste to a town of Judah, where she entered the house of Zechariah and greeted Elizabeth.

Our Blessed Mother portrays the epitome of charity as she travels to visit Elizabeth to share her joy. Conversely, we react to the crisis with anger, not charity. We are resentful and assign blame to others and to God. Jesus, anger and resentment inhibits me from accomplishing this calling. Please remove this darkness from my heart and replace it with the charity of the Blessed Mother.

My Loving Savior, Divine Caregiver, walk with me through this journey and always.

III. The Nativity

Luke 2:7: ...and she gave birth to her firstborn son. She wrapped him in swaddling clothes and laid him in a manger, because there was no room for them in the inn.

The Nativity portrays Jesus' modest beginnings and Mary and Joseph's humility. They didn't bargain with the innkeeper to displace someone else. They accepted their situation and were grateful for the shelter provided. We, in turn, try to make a deal – resisting the inevitable. We promise you Jesus, to live a better life, go to church more often, etc., if You would perform a miraculous healing.

Dear Jesus, my bargaining is not a sign of disrespect. It's an act of desperation. I do not want my loved one to suffer and I am overwhelmed by the responsibility that awaits me. Grant me the peace and serenity needed to move forward.

My Loving Savior, Divine Caregiver, walk with me through this journey and always.

IV. The Presentation

Luke 2:22: When the days were completed for their purification according to the law of Moses, they took him up to Jerusalem to present him to the Lord.

Dependence on and following our faith is so important when faced with trials; however, we are consumed with depression and fear. We are paralyzed with the feeling of impending doom. We turn away from that which can give us comfort.

Jesus, I cannot face this alone. Lift the shroud of depression and fear so I can see the never-ending light of my faith in You.

My Loving Savior, Divine Caregiver, walk with me through this journey and always.

V. The Finding of Jesus in the Temple

Luke 2:46-47: After three days they found him in the temple, sitting in the midst of the teachers, listening to them and asking them questions, and all who heard him were astounded at his understanding and his answers.

Accepting our loved one's fate is imperative if we are to be a competent and devoted caregiver. Instead of floundering in despair, we need to look for support and guidance. We need to humble ourselves and listen … listen to God and listen to those who have walked our path.

Oh Jesus, can I do this? Can I learn to be someone I was not prepared to be? Show me the way dear Jesus, and put those in my life that will give me counsel and support.

My Loving Savior, Divine Caregiver, walk with me through this journey and always.

The Luminous Mysteries

I. The Baptism in the Jordan

Matthew 3:13-16:   Then Jesus came from Galilee to John at the Jordan to be baptized by him. John tried to prevent him, saying, "I need to be baptized by you, and yet you are coming to me?" Jesus said to him in reply, "Allow it now, for thus it is fitting for us to fulfill all righteousness." Then he allowed him.

As we begin this new chapter in our lives, we will encounter unpleasant tasks, be it helping with bathing, emptying a bedpan or changing a diaper. As unpleasant as it seems to us, we need to be compassionate to our loved one. Losing independence and the ability to care for oneself is most understandably embarrassing and humiliating.

Bless me with an abundance of compassion, Dear Jesus. Please show me how, in my words and actions, to protect my loved one's dignity.

My Loving Savior, Divine Caregiver, walk with me through this journey and always.

II. The Wedding at Cana

John 2:3-7: When the wine ran short, the mother of Jesus said to him, "They have no wine." And Jesus said to her, "Woman, how does your concern affect me? My hour has not yet come." His mother said to the servers, "Do whatever he tells you. Now there were six stone water jars there for Jewish ceremonial washings, each holding twenty to thirty gallons. Jesus told them, "Fill the jars with water." So they filled them to the brim.

The wedding guests at Cana went to Mary when the wine was depleted. So should we when we, through frustration, find ourselves deficient in understanding . The Blessed Mother cared for our Lord and Savior, who best to ask for intercession?

Jesus, hear the prayers of your mother, Our Mother, to help me curb frustration and recover the understanding necessary to meet the challenges before me.

My Loving Savior, Divine Caregiver, walk with me through this journey and always.

III. The Proclamation of the Kingdom

Matthew 10:7-8:   As you go, make this proclamation: 'The kingdom of heaven is at hand.' Cure the sick, raise the dead, cleanse lepers, drive out demons. Without cost you have received; without cost you are to give.

Our loved one will feel burdensome and worthless. This will be one of our biggest challenges ... to offer reassurance that we are exactly where we want to be and doing what we want to do.

Dear Jesus, how hard it must be to be fully dependent on another, knowing the life changes that were made to accommodate the care required. Help me to impart to my loved one I consider this a wonderful opportunity to grow closer and create cherished memories.

My Loving Savior, Divine Caregiver, walk with me through this journey and always.

IV. The Transfiguration

Luke 9:29-35: While he was praying his face changed in appearance and his clothing became dazzling white. And behold, two men were conversing with him, Moses and Elijah, who appeared in glory and spoke of his exodus that he was going to accomplish in Jerusalem. Peter and his companions had been overcome by sleep, but becoming fully awake, they saw his glory and the two men standing with him. As they were about to part from him, Peter said to Jesus, "Master, it is good that we are here; let us make three tents, one for you, one for Moses, and one for Elijah." But he did not know what he was saying. While he was still speaking, a cloud came and cast a shadow over them, and they became frightened when they entered the cloud. Then from the cloud came a voice that said, "This is my chosen Son; listen to him."

God instructed Peter and his companions to listen to Jesus. We too are also instructed to listen to Jesus, which we do through prayer and meditation. We should also earnestly listen to our loved one. It has been said the eyes are the windows to the soul. Words sometimes cannot be used, but the eyes can show discomfort, fear, loneliness, etc.

Jesus, please give me the gift of hearing, not just through my ears, but through my eyes and heart.

My Loving Savior, Divine Caregiver, walk with me through this journey and always.

V. The Institution of the Eucharist

Luke 22:19-20: Then he took the bread, said the blessing, broke it, and gave it to them, saying, "This is my body, which will be given for you; do this in memory of me." And likewise the cup after they had eaten, saying, "This cup is the new covenant in my blood, which will be shed for you.

The Eucharist provides nourishment for the soul. While performing day to day tasks caring for our loved one, we can talk to God. Keeping Him ever present in our lives will bring us through the tedious and difficult times.

Jesus, keep me diligent in my prayer life. May my loved one join me in prayer and meditation and share the love and gratitude I have for You.

My Loving Savior, Divine Caregiver, walk with me through this journey and always.

The Sorrowful Mysteries

I. Agony in the Garden

Luke 22:39-42: Then going out he went, as was his custom, to the Mount of Olives, and the disciples followed him. When he arrived at the place he said to them, "Pray that you may not undergo the test." After withdrawing about a stone's throw from them and kneeling, he prayed, saying, "Father, if you are willing, take this cup away from me; still, not my will but yours be done."

The progression of illness and/or imminent death can strip away our resolve to be positive, calm and supportive. In times of weakness we need to remember Jesus in the garden. We need to turn to God for strength, ask for healing but remain steadfast in accepting His will, not ours.

Jesus, when discouragement, fear and anxiety surface, give me the resolve to stand with you as the earthbound source of comfort to my loved one. Provide me with the peace of knowing Thy will, not mine, be done.

My Loving Savior, Divine Caregiver, walk with me through this journey and always.

II. The Scourging at the Pillar

John 19:1: Then Pilate took Jesus and had him scourged.

When Jesus was scourged at the Pillar, it was an attempt to shame him and tempt Him to turn away from God. In the wake of watching our loved one struggle, we may withdraw from our faith life out of hopelessness. When we are tempted to turn away we need to intensify our conversations with God. The more we talk to Him, the hopelessness will be replaced with renewed faith and determination.

Jesus, you are my beacon of hope. Through all the pain you endured at the pillar, you never turned away from Your Father. Bless me, my loving savior, with the same fortitude and keep me close.

My Loving Savior, Divine Caregiver, walk with me through this journey and always.

III. The Crowning with Thorns

Matthew 27:27-29: Then the soldiers of the governor took Jesus inside the praetorium and gathered the whole cohort around him. They stripped off his clothes and threw a scarlet military cloak about him. Weaving a crown out of thorns, they placed it on his head, and a reed in his right hand. And kneeling before him, they mocked him, saying, "Hail, King of the Jews!"

Jesus was aware of His destiny; however, throughout his trials, did not give in. He continued to share His trust of God. Difficulties occur from time to time and we want to give up, walk away. Our patience dwindles and frustration grows. Instead of stepping back and taking time to reflect, we demean ourselves for being upset and question our capabilities.

Blessed Jesus, you know me more than I know myself, and there is a reason you entrusted me with this responsibility. May I keep that trust in the forefront of my thoughts in all my words and deeds.

My Loving Savior, Divine Caregiver, walk with me through this journey and always.

IV. The Carrying of the Cross

Luke 23:26: As they led him away they took hold of a certain Simon, a Cyrenian, who was coming in from the country; and after laying the cross on him, they made him carry it behind Jesus.

It is time for us to carry the cross of care. During our lifetime there were many moments our crosses were graciously picked up. It is important to share those moments with our loved one; impart our love and gratitude.

Jesus, the cycle of life has gone full circle. Help me carry this cross recalling those that were carried for me.

My Loving Savior, Divine Caregiver, walk with me through this journey and always.

V. The Crucifixion

Luke 23:43: He replied to him, "Amen, I say to you, today you will be with me in Paradise."

Accepting one's mortality is heartbreaking and we conceal that reality in a vain attempt to avoid the inevitable. We don't talk about it, even if our loved one wants to. We pretend not to hear, change the subject, walk away.

Jesus, we know life's journey is coming to an end. Comfort us with the knowledge that Heaven's journey follows; one so beautiful it goes beyond human comprehension.

My Loving Savior, Divine Caregiver, walk with me through this journey and always.

The Glorious Mysteries

I. The Ressurection

Mark 16:6: He said to them, "Do not be amazed! You seek Jesus of Nazareth, the crucified. He has been raised; he is not here. Behold the place where they laid him.

When the end of life comes, it will be a time of grief; however, we are told it should also be a time of rejoicing as the pain and suffering of our loved one is gone.   The thought of rejoicing is incomprehensible to us because there will be such a great void in our life.

Jesus, I know in my heart my loved one will be in a better place. Console me in my grief and as time passes, may that grief transform to joy … a celebration of how my loved one's life impacted mine, as well as many others, and of all the cherished memories we created.

My Loving Savior, Divine Caregiver, walk with me through this journey and always.

II. The Ascension

Mark 16:19: So then the Lord Jesus, after he spoke to them, was taken up into heaven and took his seat at the right hand of God.

We understood that when we took on the role of caregiver, it would end in a death. There is no way humanly possible to prepare for it emotionally. All we can do is hold true to our faith and believe our loved one, released from earthly bonds, will be with God and those that have gone before … a joyful reunion.

Beloved Jesus, may I hold true to my faith when the time comes to say goodbye. May that faith shine through the tears and give me, as well as others, comfort.

My Loving Savior, Divine Caregiver, walk with me through this journey and always.

III. The Descent of the Holy Spirit

Acts 2:1-4: When the time for Pentecost was fulfilled, they were all in one place together. And suddenly there came from the sky a noise like a strong driving wind, and it filled the entire house in which they were. Then there appeared to them tongues as of fire, which parted and came to rest on each one of them. And they were all filled with the Holy Spirit and began to speak in different tongues, as the Spirit enabled them to proclaim.

The Holy Spirit descended on us the minute we took on the responsibility of care-giving to give us hope, love and compassion. It will continue to live within us when our job is done, to give us strength and peace.

Jesus, I sometimes feel so alone, contemplating the present and the future. Open my heart and soul to feel the presence of the Holy Spirit freeing me of isolation.

My Loving Savior, Divine Caregiver, walk with me through this journey and always.

IV. The Assumption

1 Corinthians 6:17: But whoever is joined to the Lord becomes one spirit with him.

We struggle with the thought of our loved one's passing and worry we'll weaken in grief and renounce all that we believe. Will we do the unthinkable and question the existence of God and Heaven? It's possible. Grief can cause a multitude of contrary thoughts but be assured God will not forsake us, even at our worst.

All loving and forgiving Jesus, be with me when I struggle with the doubts grief can spawn. Remind me of the Assumption's message....Heaven exists and when life ends on earth, our loved one will be one in spirit with our Father.

My Loving Savior, Divine Caregiver, walk with me through this journey and always.

V. The Coronation

Revelation 12:1: A great sign appeared in the sky, a woman clothed with the sun, with the moon under her feet, and on her head a crown of twelve stars.

In our mission, our loved one looks to us for care until Heaven calls. How glorious, that at that minute, the mission will be reversed. Just as we ask for Blessed Mother, Queen of Heaven's intercession, we can ask the same of our loved one. And we will pray:

Our Loving God and Savior, please hear my prayers through the intercession of the Blessed Mother and your newest angel.

My Loving Savior, Divine Caregiver, walk with me through this journey and always.

Redeemed
Rosary Meditations
for
Post-Abortive Women

Patti J. Smith

For Sarah and Matthew ~ My Angels
I swept you away so long ago;
I tried to move on, to forget.
I continued my life as if nothing occurred,
ignoring the regret.

Feelings of anguish would surface,
which I couldn't understand.
I would shrug it off, chalk it up to life,
just issues to withstand.

I didn't know that it was you,
opening my eyes to see,
That you wanted to be remembered
as a special part of me.

The sadness grew and followed me,
no matter how hard I tried to run.
There was nowhere else to go;
my life had come undone.

Finally reaching out for hope,
I learned the reason for my strife.
I hadn't mourned for what was swept
so quickly from my life,

I didn't know that it was you,
opening my eyes to see,
But now you are remembered
and are a forever part of me.

Introduction

Regardless of the circumstances surrounding an unplanned pregnancy, there is something women may not be aware of when they decide on abortion; the emotional, physical and spiritual consequences. At first there is a sense of relief; however, a few months, years, or decades later the effects may surface with disastrous results.

The physical side-effects of abortion can be dealt with medically; however, this devotional will focus on healing the soul. Women carrying the burden of guilt and shame of abortion may turn to drugs, alcohol and promiscuity to hide the pain. Others suffer from depression and might contemplate suicide. They may have many failed relationships, not want children, or resist bonding with the children they bear. If they were spiritual or religious, leaving the church and their faith community could result due to a feeling of being undeserving of God's presence in their lives.

There is hope, there is healing. Nothing is unforgivable. God is merciful and loves us. He sees our tears and our pain and wants to hold us in His comforting arms. He wants us to talk to Him, ask His forgiveness, and welcome Him back into our lives. He wants us to be closer to His mother, the Blessed Virgin Mary as she, above all, knows the pain of loss.

These meditations are for all women who have suffered the pain of abortion. I pray they provide peace and comfort and encourage a stronger relationship to God and the Blessed Mother.

The Joyful Mysteries

I. The Annunciation

Luke 1:34-38 But Mary said to the angel, "How can this be, since I have no relations with a man?" And the angel said to her in reply, "The holy Spirit will come upon you, and the power of the Most High will overshadow you. Therefore the child to be born will be called holy, the Son of God. And behold, Elizabeth, your relative, has also conceived a son in her old age, and this is the sixth month for her who was called barren; for nothing will be impossible for God." Mary said, "Behold, I am the handmaid of the Lord. May it be done to me according to your word." Then the angel departed from her.

When Mary was visited by the angel, she was apprehensive; however, because of her deep faith, she said, "Yes". She was willing to do the Lord's bidding and knew that nothing is impossible for God.

An unplanned pregnancy is complicated. There are so many emotions involved. There is fear, anxiety and embarrassment. Sometimes there is joy; however, with disappointment and pressure of family, friends and significant others, the joy turns to dismay...weakness prevails and a decision to abort is made.

Jesus, I am so sorry I said, "No". My faith was weak and my soul was heavy. I look back and wish I had taken the path of the Blessed Mother. I should have known you would never abandon me in my time of need. Isaiah 41:10 tells us, "For I am the Lord, your God, who grasp your right hand; it is I who say to you, do not fear, I will help you".

I rejected Your promise and my child and although I felt deserving of nothing but the fires of hell, You forgave me. How humbling it is to be forgiven for something so egregious.

Sweet Jesus and Blessed Mother, I commit my child to your loving care until our glorious reunion in Heaven.

II. The Visitation

Luke 1:41-42: "...and Elizabeth, filled with the Holy Spirit, cried out in a loud voice and said, "Most blessed are you among women, and blessed is the fruit of your womb."

Jesus, you were blessed at conception as all children. Why couldn't I see that? I tried so hard to pretend it wasn't real; it was just tissue and not a child. I convinced myself I was doing the right thing, and ignored the doubts I had in my mind. I felt if I just "took care of it", I could get on with my life...out of sight, out of mind.

My child may have been out of sight; however, not out of mind. That precious being was part of me from the day of conception and although I was not conscious of it, was trying to speak to me. I could not hear that little voice and did everything in my power to ignore it.

I know now, my wonderful Jesus, that through Your mercy, my child never left my mind. You gave me the opportunity to bring

my angel into my life forever, with anticipation of a heavenly reunion.

Sweet Jesus and Blessed Mother, I commit my child to your loving care until our glorious reunion in Heaven.

III. The Nativity

Luke 2:6-7: While they were there, the time came for her to have her child, and she gave birth to her firstborn son. She wrapped him in swaddling clothes and laid him in a manger, because there was no room for them in the inn.

Jesus, your first bed was a manger, in a stable; a humble beginning. The Blessed Mother, no matter what the accommodations, made sure you had everything you needed to be safe and secure.

My child may have had a humble beginning as well but instead of trusting in You and myself, I gave in to pressure and fear. I pretended I was protecting my child from a life of poverty, being branded a "mistake", or any other perceived consequence of being unplanned. I was wrong in my perceptions.

Jesus, I can't turn back time but through Your forgiveness and mercy I am able to move forward and help others to see the truth through my experience.

Sweet Jesus and Blessed Mother, I commit my child to your loving care until our glorious reunion in Heaven.

IV. The Presentation of Jesus

Luke 2:33-34: The child's father and mother were amazed at what was said about him; and Simeon blessed them and said to Mary his mother, "Behold, this child is destined for the fall

and rise of many in Israel, and to be a sign that will be contradicted."

Jesus, every child conceived has a destiny. Who was I to reject Your will and take that away? My child would have brought joy to my life as well as the lives of others and done so much if given the chance. The reality of taking that earthly future away, the opportunity to grow, learn and be loved, is excruciating. It's only through Your grace I find comfort, as I know my child has a heavenly future with You.

Sweet Jesus and Blessed Mother, I commit my child to your loving care until our glorious reunion in Heaven.

V. The Finding of Jesus in the Temple

Luke 2:43-45: ..Jesus remained behind in Jerusalem, but his parents did not know it. Thinking that he was in the caravan, they journeyed for a day and looked for him among their relatives and acquaintances, but not finding him, they returned to Jerusalem to look for him.

Jesus, I have had dreams of endless searches for a lost child. The ache in my heart and panic was so frightening real, I would awaken in tears gasping for breath.

I believe You sent those dreams as a reminder of what I lost and to show me my child existed. The dreams are not punishment but a way to bring that child into my heart.

Sweet Jesus and Blessed Mother, I commit my child to your loving care until our glorious reunion in Heaven.

The Luminous Mysteries

I. The Baptism in the Jordan

Matthew 3:17: And a voice from heaven said, "This is my Son, the Beloved, with whom I am well pleased".

Jesus, I know my decision to abort did not please you. My own priorities were more important and the wonderful blessing you bestowed upon me was considered inconvenient. I didn't listen to you then because I knew you would guide me in a direction I was not courageous enough to take.

Being one of your beloved, You must have shed many tears for me and my child. I pray I am able to dry Your tears by repenting and holding my child close to my heart.

Sweet Jesus and Blessed Mother, I commit my child to your loving care until our glorious reunion in Heaven.

II. The Wedding at Cana

John 2:2-5: Jesus and his disciples had also been invited to the wedding. When the wine gave out, the mother of Jesus said to him, "They have no wine." And Jesus said to her, "Woman, what concern is that to you and to me? My hour has not yet come." His mother said to the servants, "Do whatever he tells you."

Our Blessed Mother knew that her son would perform a miracle for the wedding celebration to continue. Knowing how miraculous Jesus was and is, how could I have ever doubted Him or ignored His desires for me?

Jesus, I know I failed you with my doubts and for that I suffered a great deal of shame and remorse. Thank you for helping me understand that you know my heart and forgave me; that although my actions were not of God, they too can be turned miraculous by being witness to others.

Sweet Jesus and Blessed Mother, I commit my child to your loving care until our glorious reunion in Heaven.

III. The Proclamation of the Kingdom

Matthew 5:1-4: When Jesus saw the crowds, he went up to the mountain; and after he sat down, his disciples came to him. Then he began to speak, and taught them, saying: "blessed are the poor in spirit, for theirs is the kingdom of heaven. Blessed are those who mourn, for they will be comforted."

Jesus, I know when I first aborted my child I believed I wasn't in mourning. I lied to myself and to others that I was comfortable with my actions and that I was, in fact, relieved. That lie festered in me until I could no longer ignore it. I was mourning from the first but would not listen to my heart. I buried the pain so deep in my soul, it would take years to surface; only then did I mourn and all the tears that had been welled up for so long flowed like a raging river.

Again my loving Savior, you didn't fail me. You provided the comfort and understanding I needed in order to reconcile with my past and move forward in faith.

Sweet Jesus and Blessed Mother, I commit my child to your loving care until our glorious reunion in Heaven.

IV. The Transfiguration

Luke 9:33-36:   Just as they were leaving him, Peter said to Jesus, "Master, it is good for us to be here; let us make three dwellings, one for you, one for Moses, and one for Elijah" – not knowing what he said. While he was saying this, a cloud came and overshadowed them; and they were terrified as they entered the cloud. Then from the cloud came a voice that said, "This is my son, my Chosen; listen to him!" When the voice had spoken, Jesus was found alone. And they kept silent and in those days told no one any of the things they had seen.

Listening to Jesus and following my heart was not something I was willing to do. I chose to go against God's will for me and take the coward's path of fear and selfishness. I did not want to accept responsibility for myself or for my child.

Jesus, I know you spoke to me but I closed my heart. Your words lingered over me like a beacon in the dark, to be reached out to and enlightened. I stayed in the darkness and remained there because I believed I belonged there. I now bask in Your light, the light of love, mercy and forgiveness. With your help, I will try each day to keep the dark clouds of doubt and fear at bay.

Sweet Jesus and Blessed Mother, I commit my child to your loving care until our glorious reunion in Heaven.

V. The Institution of the Eucharist

I Corinthians 11: 23-26: For I received from the Lord what I also handed on to you, that the Lord Jesus on the night when he was betrayed took a loaf of bread, and when he had given thanks, he broke it and said, "This is my body that is for you. Do this in remembrance of me." In the same way he took the cup also, after supper, saying, "This cup is the new covenant in my blood. Do this, as often as you drink it, in remembrance of me. For as often, as you eat this bread and drink the cup, you proclaim the Lord's death until he comes.

Jesus, how many of us have strayed from our faith because we felt undeserving to be in Your house as well as feast at Your table. The guilt and shame kept us from Your lifesaving blood and body. So grateful am I, that through taking my great sin to the sacrament of Reconciliation you blessed me with Your unconditional mercy and absolution. I rejoice at being welcomed at Your table to remember all You sacrificed for me.

Sweet Jesus and Blessed Mother, I commit my child to your loving care until our glorious reunion in Heaven.

The Sorrowful Mysteries

I. Agony in the Garden

Matthew 26:40:   When he returned to his disciples he found them asleep. He said to Peter, "So you could not keep watch with me for one hour?"

Jesus, I know the sadness you must have had in your heart when no one stayed awake with you. After that precious life was swept away from me I may have had family, friends or significant others around me, but I was so very alone in my agony. I was in a private hell that was so painful I buried it with whatever would keep it hidden...alcohol, drugs, men. I wanted to forget there was a life and soul lost; not just my child's, but mine as well.

Thank you Jesus for bringing me back from hell, from being shrouded in agony. Thank you for freeing me from my excesses and bringing me closer to You.

Sweet Jesus and Blessed Mother, I commit my child to your loving care until our glorious reunion in Heaven.

II. The Scourging at the Pillar

John 19:1: Then Pilate took Jesus and had him scourged.

Jesus, you were unmercifully punished and one can only imagine the pain you endured; you were an innocent. I was not an innocent so I punished myself. I purposely ruined

relationships, not allowing anyone to get close to me. I isolated my heart from the children I did bear or became so protective of them, they retreated from me. I was a muddled mess of emotions that could not be contained or controlled.

I am so grateful Jesus, that You freed me from self-punishment and certain insanity.

Sweet Jesus and Blessed Mother, I commit my child to your loving care until our glorious reunion in Heaven.

III. The Crowning With Thorns

John 19:2-4: And the soldiers wove a crown out of thorns and placed it on his head, and clothed him in a purple cloak, and they came to him and said, "Hail, King of the Jews!" And they struck him repeatedly. Once more Pilate went out and said to them, "Look, I am bringing him out to you, so that you may know that I find no guilt in him."

Although Pilate found no guilt in Jesus, he was pressured by the Jews to condemn Him. Jesus, I pressured myself into condemnation. I was immersed in guilt, shame and self-hatred. I did not deserve to be alive; I wanted to die, and I did. Day by day, year to year, I let those emotions steal away every last ounce of hope and happiness. I was an empty shell.

Jesus, through your love and mercy, I am no longer condemned. My life is renewed and hope and happiness is within reach.

Sweet Jesus and Blessed Mother, I commit my child to your loving care until our glorious reunion in Heaven.

IV. The Carrying of the Cross

John 19:17:   ...and carrying the cross himself he went out to what is called the Place of the Skull, in Hebrew, Golgotha.

My wonderful Lord, I carried my cross alone too, but for a different reason. I did it by choice. I didn't turn to You to carry that burden. I let myself suffer in silence and alone. I felt the burden of abortion was one deserved to be carried solely by me.

Jesus, help me to be the example that demonstrates no cross, even abortion, is too heavy to be carried by You. Allow me the privilege to carry their cross with You.

Sweet Jesus and Blessed Mother, I commit my child to your loving care until our glorious reunion in Heaven.

V. The Crucifixion

Luke 23:34: Then Jesus said, "Father, forgive them, they know not what they do."

Jesus, unlike those who crucified you, I knew what I did; however, I was not willing to admit to myself I took the life of an innocent child. I was living a lie. I was blind to the blessing you bestowed upon me and deaf to the pleas of my little one.

Jesus, I made a devastating choice but through Your grace, can accept responsibility for what I did. I know, deep down in my soul, that You have forgiven me because You know my heart and can see the pain and remorse.

Sweet Jesus and Blessed Mother, I commit my child to your loving care until our glorious reunion in Heaven.

The Glorious Mysteries

I. The Resurrection

Luke 24:13-16: Now that very day two of them were going to a village seven miles from Jerusalem called Emmaus, and they were conversing about all the things that had occurred. And it happened that while they were conversing and debating, Jesus himself drew near and walked with them, but their eyes were prevented from recognizing him.

Jesus, my eyes also were prevented from recognizing You and it was because I chose not to see. I was blinded by fear and selfishness. My faith was non-existent. I could not see that what You gave me was a gift to be loved and cherished. Thank you for removing the dark veil from my eyes and allowing me to see You and see the beauty of Your creations.

Sweet Jesus and Blessed Mother, I commit my child to your loving care until our glorious reunion in Heaven.

II. The Ascension

Luke 24:50-51: Then he led them as far as Bethany, raised his hands, and blessed them. As he blessed them he parted from them and was taken up to heaven.

Through Your healing power Jesus, I have acknowledged my child. I am in such ecstasy knowing my angel has been freed from my secret and is watching over me.

Sweet Jesus and Blessed Mother, I commit my child to your loving care until our glorious reunion in Heaven.

III. The Descent of the Holy Spirit

Acts 2:1-4: When the time for Pentecost was fulfilled, they were all in one place together. And suddenly there came from the sky a noise like a strong driving wind, and it filled the entire house in which they were. Then there appeared to them tongues as of fire, which parted and came to rest on each one of them. And they were all filled with the holy Spirit and began to speak in different tongues, as the Spirit enabled them to proclaim.

Jesus, how blessed I am that You sent the Holy Spirit to fill me with hope and tranquility. Through all the pain and suffering I was a shell. Empty, hopeless, ashamed. I was nothing. I am now filled not only with the Holy Spirit, but with the spirit of my child of which both sustain me. I will never be alone again.

Sweet Jesus and Blessed Mother, I commit my child to your loving care until our glorious reunion in Heaven.

IV. The Assumption of Mary

Revelation 12:5: She gave birth to a son, a male child, destined to rule all the nations with an iron rod. Her child was caught up to God and his throne.

Our Blessed Mother Mary was assumed into heaven, body and soul, because she was free of sin and the perfect mother. She set the example for all women; however, I ignored her. Mother Mary, thank you for loving my child and for loving me until I was able to do it myself. Thank you for your constant intercession and for showing me how precious life is, at conception and beyond.

Sweet Jesus and Blessed Mother, I commit my child to your loving care until our glorious reunion in Heaven.

V. The Coronation of Mary

Revelation 12:1: A great sign appeared in the sky, a woman clothed with the sun, with the moon under her feet, and on her head a crown of twelve stars.

Mary is the mother of God, Queen of Heaven and Earth. She holds all of God's children in her arms and loves them with a love that extends beyond earthly bounds. I rejoice knowing my child is with her, and can only imagine what it will be like to have her gently place that beautiful miracle back in my arms.

Sweet Jesus and Blessed Mother, I commit my child to your loving care until our glorious reunion in Heaven.

Acknowledgements

A few years ago, I attended a "Life in the Spirit" seminar. Although I was getting my life on track, something was still amiss and I was desperately searching for answers. One of the speakers was a woman that shared her abortion experience and the emotional and spiritual turmoil that followed. She spoke of a post-abortion healing retreat she attended, Rachel's Hope, and how it put the pieces of her life together. God spoke to me through her that day. My tears flowed while she shared. It was as if she was pulling her words out of my heart. **I found the answer**.

Rachel's Hope helped me uncover the shame, pain and self-loathing that had been buried deep within my soul for decades. I was finally able to come to terms with what I had done and ask God and my children for forgiveness. I was also able to forgive myself and be free from the inconsolable anguish.

Thank you, Leslie Brunolli, for sharing your story of hope and starting me on this wonderful journey. Asking me to work with you in facilitating retreats gives me the opportunity to witness healing in others and inspires me to continue sharing my testimony in order to reach those in need. You are such an inspiration to me as well as many others.

Rosemary Benefield, your boundless love, encouragement and gentle guidance during that retreat rescued me. You turned the pain and suffering I was experiencing into something from which I could learn and grow. The program you and your wonderful husband Jim created has not only brought me, but so many other women, hope and peace through God's mercy.

Talk to Jesus

The world is changing quickly,
it's filled with pain and strife.
But Jesus won't desert you,
He saved you with His life.

Don't let the pain confuse you,
don't let the hate control
the way you think you need to live,
don't let it take your soul.

They'll try to make you waiver,
to see the pain upon your face.
But know no matter what they do
you'll have our Father's grace.

They'll want to make you fearful
and try to make you stray,
but none of that will happen
if you turn to Him and pray.

Hit your knees and talk to Jesus,
He'll listen, wait and see.
Open up your heart to Him,
and He will set you free.

Introduction

Life is teeming with obligations and activities. At times we become overwhelmed; we lose track of priorities.

The foremost priority, our relationship with God, unfortunately gets lost in the chaos. We put off praying for a quieter time, we miss church in order to relax and that cycle continues.

Curiously, what we don't realize is that if we maintain our daily relationship with God, all things will fall into place. *Psalms 107:29-30* makes it perfectly clear, *"He hushed the storm to silence,the waves of the sea were stilled. They rejoiced that the sea grew calm, that God brought them to the harbor they longed for."*

Regardless of how busy we are, if we start the day conversing with God, he will still the storm before it begins or give us the strength to withstand it. If we end the day thanking God, we will retire serenely, becoming refreshed to Embrace the Morning.

The Joyful Mysteries

I. The Annunciation

Luke 1:38: Mary said, "Behold, I am the handmaid of the Lord. May it be done to me according to your word." Then the angel departed from her.

Being open to God's will is sometimes quite difficult. In our hearts we want to; however, our minds manipulate us into going the opposite direction. We need to be cognizant that Satan is always close by and is waiting for self-will to take control. Once that happens, he is free to create havoc and discontent in our lives.

To differentiate between God's will and our own, we are given subtle clues. These clues can appear as an uneasy feeling in the pit of our stomach or an odd feeling of impending disaster.

Jesus, self-will runs riot in my life. It is so easy to take the reins myself thinking I am in control. Keep me ever mindful that You would never lead me astray; that you love me and want only what is best for my life.

My Precious Savior, guide me to follow Your word in my thoughts, words and deeds. At day's end may I count my blessings with love and gratitude.

II. The Visitation

Luke 1:41-44:   When Elizabeth heard Mary's greeting, the infant leaped in her womb, and Elizabeth, filled with the holy Spirit, cried out in a loud voice and said, "Most blessed are you among women, and blessed is the fruit of your womb. And how does this happen to me, that the mother of my Lord should come to me? For at the moment the sound of your greeting reached my ears, the infant in my womb leaped for joy".

The visitation shares the message of Mary's unselfishness by traveling a great distance while pregnant to see Elizabeth; however, it also shares the message that we need to rejoice in the Lord. It is our calling as Christians to spread His word. The current atmosphere in our world makes us reluctant to discuss faith at school, the workplace or other arenas; however, we can do it and God wants us to. If we don't share our joy in Christ we have lost the wonderful opportunity to bring others to Him.

Jesus, I love you and want others to love you as well. Bless me with opportunities to open Your door to non-believers.

My Precious Savior, guide me to follow Your word in my thoughts, words and deeds. At day's end may I count my blessings with love and gratitude.

III. The Nativity

Luke 2: 8-14:   Now there were shepherds in that region living in the fields and keeping the night watch over their flock. The angel of the Lord appeared to them and the glory of the Lord shone around them, and they were struck with great fear. The angel said to them, "Do not be afraid; for behold, I proclaim to you good news of great joy that will be for all the people. For today in the city of David a savior has been born for you who is Messiah and Lord. And this will be a sign for you: you will find an infant wrapped in swaddling clothes and lying in a manger." And suddenly there was a multitude of the heavenly host with the angel, praising God and saying: "Glory to God in the highest and on earth peace to those on whom his favor rests."

Can you imagine what life would be like if Jesus had not been born? We would be like lost sheep, with no direction. Through Him we found our Father … through Him we know how to live righteously … through Him we can have eternal life.

Blessed Mother, your faithfulness to God brought us a savior and I am filled with gratitude. Without Him, I would be adrift in a world void of purpose and filled with hopelessness. Heavenly Father, through Your son I have been saved and pray I can follow his path of righteousness.

My Precious Savior, guide me to follow Your word in my thoughts, words and deeds. At day's end may I count my blessings with love and gratitude.

IV. The Presentation

Luke 2:22: When the days were completed for their purification according to the law of Moses, they took him up to Jerusalem to present him to the Lord.

We too need to present ourselves to the Lord through prayer and meditation. He knows we are here, but wants us to talk to Him and focus on His word. Through our quiet time with Him we are renewed in spirit and ready to face our daily challenges head-on.

Father, forgive me for the times I have failed to present myself. May I become rededicated to set aside quiet time with you in prayer and meditation.

My Precious Savior, guide me to follow Your word in my thoughts, words and deeds. At day's end may I count my blessings with love and gratitude.

V. The Finding of Jesus in the Temple

Luke 2: 49-52: And he said to them, "Why were you looking for me? Did you not know that I must be in my Father's house?" But they did not understand what he said to them. He went down with them and came to Nazareth, and was obedient to them; and his mother kept all these things in her heart. And Jesus advanced in wisdom and age and favor before God and man.

We too find ourselves searching for God, but all we have to do is open our eyes and hearts to see the blessings he has granted us – not only from within. Look around - see the beauty He has created. The magnificent sunrises and sunsets, the exquisiteness of nature.

My dearest Father, you have created a world of beauty and wonder. May my eyes and heart focus on that beauty and know You are ever present in my life.

My Precious Savior, guide me to follow Your word in my thoughts, words and deeds. At day's end may I count my blessings with love and gratitude.

The Luminous Mysteries

I. The Baptism in the Jordan

Matthew 3:13-17: Then Jesus came from Galilee to John at the Jordan to be baptized by him. John tried to prevent him, saying, "I need to be baptized by you, and yet you are coming to me?" Jesus said to him in reply, "Allow it now, for thus it is fitting for us to fulfill all righteousness." Then he allowed him. After Jesus was baptized, he came up from the water and behold, the heavens were opened, and he saw the Spirit of God descending like a dove coming upon him. And a voice came from the heavens, saying, "This is my beloved Son, with whom I am well pleased."

Jesus' baptism in the Jordan shows us that humility needs to be a constant in our life. We should not center our lives on receiving praise and admiration. If we are secure in our faith, our identity will be based on the love of God, not the opinion of others.

Jesus, just as you showed great humility at your baptism, so should I in everything I do. May I always remember my inspiration for all endeavors should not be the opinions of others but the unconditional love of God.

My Precious Savior, guide me to follow Your word in my thoughts, words and deeds. At day's end may I count my blessings with love and gratitude.

II. The Wedding at Cana

John 2:11: Jesus did this as the beginning of his signs in Cana in Galilee and so revealed his glory, and his disciples began to believe in him.

Miracles surround us – not only visually. Hearing the ocean crash against the rocks, thunder that brings refreshing rain, a bird singing, the cry of a newborn child. The beautiful music of life.

Most gracious Jesus, may I always hold a sense of wonder and joy in the miracles before me.

My Precious Savior, guide me to follow Your word in my thoughts, words and deeds. At day's end may I count my blessings with love and gratitude.

III. The Proclamation of the Kingdom

Matthew 5:1-10:   When he saw the crowds, he went up the mountain, and after he had sat down, his disciples came to him. He began to teach them, saying: "Blessed are the poor in spirit, for theirs is the kingdom of heaven. Blessed are they who mourn, for they will be comforted. Blessed are the meek, for they will inherit the land. Blessed are they who hunger and thirst for righteousness, for they will be satisfied. Blessed are the merciful, for they will be shown mercy. Blessed are the clean of heart, for they will see God. Blessed are the peacemakers, for they will be called children of God. Blessed are they who are persecuted for the sake of righteousness, for theirs is the kingdom of heaven.

The Beatitudes show us the path to Heaven. They invite us to walk with God and live a life serving Him and others. They give us a moral compass.

Dear Jesus, Your words show me the way to salvation. May I do all in my power to keep them close to my heart and abide by them always.

My Precious Savior, guide me to follow Your word in my thoughts, words and deeds. At day's end may I count my blessings with love and gratitude.

IV. The Transfiguration

Matthew 9: 2-8: After six days Jesus took Peter, James, and John and led them up a high mountain apart by themselves. And he was transfigured before them, and his clothes became dazzling white, such as no fuller on earth could bleach them. Then Elijah appeared to them along with Moses, and they were conversing with Jesus. Then Peter said to Jesus in reply, "Rabbi, it is good that we are here! Let us make three tents: one for you, one for Moses, and one for Elijah." He hardly knew what to say, they were so terrified. Then a cloud came, casting a shadow over them; then from the cloud came a voice, "This is my beloved Son. Listen to him." Suddenly, looking around, they no longer saw anyone but Jesus alone with them.

When we feel lost, confused or anxious there is serenity in Jesus. All we need to do is be still and pray. In the stillness of prayer we will be calmed.

Jesus, your Father wants me to turn to You, not just in times of joy but also of distress. May I follow His bidding and know you will take my distress and replace it with tranquility.

My Precious Savior, guide me to follow Your word in my thoughts, words and deeds. At day's end may I count my blessings with love and gratitude.

V. The Institution of the Eucharist

John 6:32-35: So Jesus said to them, "Amen, amen, I say to you, it was not Moses who gave the bread from heaven; my Father gives you the true bread from heaven. For the bread of God is that which comes down from heaven and gives life to the world." So they said to him, "Sir, give us this bread always." Jesus said to them, "I am the bread of life; whoever comes to me will never hunger, and whoever believes in me will never thirst.

In order to physically survive, we need nourishment. The same applies to spiritual survival. We need the body and blood of Christ to nourish our souls. His nourishment give us hope, love and a purpose to our lives.

Lamb of God, through Your life saving body and blood, I will never hunger or thirst for spiritual nourishment. May I remain devoted to joining You at the banquet of life.

My Precious Savior, guide me to follow Your word in my thoughts, words and deeds. At day's end may I count my blessings with love and gratitude.

The Sorrowful Mysteries

I. Agony in the Garden

Luke 22:39-42: Then going out he went, as was his custom, to the Mount of Olives, and the disciples followed him. When he arrived at the place he said to them, "Pray that you may not undergo the test." After withdrawing about a stone's throw from them and kneeling, he prayed, saying, "Father, if you are willing, take this cup away from me; still, not my will but yours be done.

Jesus, in his agony, remained steadfast in accepting the Father's will. We too are faced with agony in our life and need to hold fast to the belief that God is with us. He will not saddle us with more than we can endure. In His mercy, he will give us the fortitude to withstand anything that comes our way – **if we let Him**.

Jesus, in your agony you turned to the Father in faith and trust, knowing he would never forsake you. When I am faced with challenges in my life, may my faith and trust emulate yours.

My Precious Savior, guide me to follow Your word in my thoughts, words and deeds. At day's end may I count my blessings with love and gratitude.

II. The Scourging at the Pillar

John 19:1: Then Pilate took Jesus and had him scourged.

Although Jesus suffered excruciating pain, He never once let go of His love for us or his persecutors. Our hearts break for the pain he endured but conversely we should rejoice in His abundance of love. We need to follow His example by loving one another, despite any transgression against us.

Jesus, no amount of pain stopped You from loving me. When I am faced with pain or cruelty from others, may I not lash out in anger, but respond with love.

My Precious Savior, guide me to follow Your word in my thoughts, words and deeds. At day's end may I count my blessings with love and gratitude.

III. The Crowning of Thorns

Matthew 27:27-31: Then the soldiers of the governor took Jesus inside the praetorium and gathered the whole cohort around him. They stripped off his clothes and threw a scarlet military cloak about him. Weaving a crown out of thorns, they placed it on his head, and a reed in his right hand. And kneeling before him, they mocked him, saying, "Hail, King of the Jews!" They spat upon him and took the reed and kept striking him on the head. And when they had mocked him, they stripped him of the cloak, dressed him in his own clothes, and led him off to crucify him.

The crowning of thorns was something to humiliate Jesus into renouncing his faith, but faith prevailed. There are individuals in our world that mock us and attempt to lead us astray. We need to be diligent in maintaining a strong relationship with God, thus our faith too will prevail.

My sweet Jesus, your crown of thorns is not one of humiliation but one of victory. Victory over Your tormentors through unwavering faith. When I am mocked and tempted, grant me the same unwavering faith so I can join You in victory.

My Precious Savior, guide me to follow Your word in my thoughts, words and deeds. At day's end may I count my blessings with love and gratitude.

IV. The Carrying of the Cross

John 19:17: ...and carrying the cross himself he went out to what is called the Place of the Skull, in Hebrew, Golgotha.

Jesus willingly carried His cross, bearing the full weight of our sins. To reciprocate, we must pick up our crosses and follow in His footsteps and spread the word of God's love and mercy.

Jesus, carrying my cross and following you should not be a burden but a joy – because I know regardless how heavy my cross may become, You are there, carrying it with me.

My Precious Savior, guide me to follow Your word in my thoughts, words and deeds. At day's end may I count my blessings with love and gratitude.

V. The Crucifixion

Luke 23:46: Jesus cried out in a loud voice, "Father, into your hands I commend my spirit"; and when he had said this he breathed his last.

Jesus died for us. He made the ultimate sacrifice to save our souls. Because of His sacrifice, we can have eternal salvation if we are obedient to His teachings. We should replace selfish desires with good works, confess our sins and repent, and share Jesus' love with others.

Jesus, help me to become more obedient. Guide me in good works and sharing Your love. Give me the capacity to acknowledge my sins and be repentant.

My Precious Savior, guide me to follow Your word in my thoughts, words and deeds. At day's end may I count my blessings with love and gratitude.

The Glorious Mysteries

I. The Resurrection

Mark 16: 6: He said to them, "Do not be amazed! You seek Jesus of Nazareth, the crucified. He has been raised; he is not here. Behold the place where they laid him.

The resurrection brought a new beginning to our world. A world of hope for the future. We can experience a faith resurrection each morning, by turning our lives over to God and accepting His will.

Jesus, You brought light into my world by rising from the tomb. May that light live within me and may I joyfully share it with those in darkness.

My Precious Savior, guide me to follow Your word in my thoughts, words and deeds. At day's end may I count my blessings with love and gratitude.

II. The Ascension

Mark 16:19: So then the Lord Jesus, after he spoke to them, was taken up into heaven and took his seat at the right hand of God.

Jesus' ascension represents His earthly work was done; however, the work of His disciples was just beginning ... to share the word of God and bring others to His mercy. And so it is with us. We too are His disciples and are blessed with the task of continuing His work.

Dear Jesus, you earned your heavenly reward by spreading the word of God and for sacrificing Your life for our sins. With Your loving help, may I become Your faithful and loyal disciple and at life's end, be welcomed into Your kingdom.

My Precious Savior, guide me to follow Your word in my thoughts, words and deeds. At day's end may I count my blessings with love and gratitude.

III. The Descent of the Holy Spirit

Acts 2:   When the time for Pentecost was fulfilled, they were all in one place together. And suddenly there came from the sky a noise like a strong driving wind, and it filled the entire house in which they were. Then there appeared to them tongues as of fire, which parted and came to rest on each one of them. And they were all filled with the holy Spirit and began to speak in different tongues, as the Spirit enabled them to proclaim.

In our lives of discipleship, there will be days when we are downtrodden and discouraged. We become complacent and tempted by selfish endeavors.

Heavenly Father, when I become discouraged, send down the Holy Spirit to restore my enthusiasm to carry out my mission with joy and zeal.

My Precious Savior, guide me to follow Your word in my thoughts, words and deeds. At day's end may I count my blessings with love and gratitude.

IV. The Assumption

Luke 1:30: Then the angel said to her, "Do not be afraid, Mary, for you have found favor with God.

Our Blessed Mother was assumed into Heaven as a reward for her unadulterated faith and obedience to God. Her assumption give us hope for life in Heaven if we follow her course.

Heavenly Father, I do my best to be faithful and obedient but outside temptations are strong. Give me the strength to withstand temptation and follow the example of Blessed Mother Mary.

My Precious Savior, guide me to follow Your word in my thoughts, words and deeds. At day's end may I count my blessings with love and gratitude.

V. The Coronation

Revelation 12:1: A great sign appeared in the sky, a woman clothed with the sun, with the moon under her feet, and on her head a crown of twelve stars.

When the Blessed Mother was assumed into Heaven, we were blessed with an intercessory. She is a protector, a guardian. She is our Mother and she wants us to draw near to her in times of need. We should also go to her in thanksgiving for her uncompromising faith and undaunted willingness to be the Mother of God.

Blessed Mother, your faith and love of God was immeasurable and your reward much deserved. Pray for me dear Mother, that my faith reaches the depth of yours ... as I my longing at life's end is to be united with you and our Father in Heaven.

My Precious Savior, guide me to follow Your word in my thoughts, words and deeds. At day's end may I count my blessings with love and gratitude.

How To Pray The Rosary

❖ While holding the crucifix, make the SIGN OF THE CROSS: "In the name of the Father, and of the Son and of the Holy Spirit. Amen."

❖ Then, recite the APOSTLE'S CREED:

"I BELIEVE IN GOD, the Father almighty, Creator of heaven and earth, and in Jesus Christ his only Son, our Lord, who was conceived by the Holy Spirit, born of the Virgin Mary, suffered under Pontius Pilate, was crucified, died and was buried; he descended into hell; on the third day he rose again from the dead; he ascended into h heaven, and is seated at the right hand of God the Father almighty; from there he will come to judge the living and the dead. I believe in the Holy Spirit, the holy catholic Church, the communion of saints, the forgiveness of sins, the resurrection of the body, and life everlasting. Amen."

❖ Recite the OUR FATHER, on the first large bead:

"OUR FATHER, Who art in heaven, Hallowed be Thy Name. Thy Kingdom come. Thy will be done, on earth as it is in heaven. Give us this day our daily bread. Forgive us our trespasses as we forgive those who trespass against us. And lead us not into temptation, but deliver us from evil. Amen."

❖ On each of the three small beads, recite a HAIL MARY

"HAIL MARY, full of grace, the Lord is with thee; Blessed art thou among women, and blessed is the fruit of thy womb, Jesus. Holy Mary, Mother of God, pray for us sinners, now and at the hour of our death. Amen."

❖ Recite the GLORY BE on the next large bead.

"GLORY BE to the Father, and to the Son, and to the Holy Spirit. As it was in the beginning, is now and ever shall be, world without end. Amen."

❖ Recall the first Rosary Mystery and recite the Our Father on the next large bead.

❖ On each of the adjacent ten small beads (known as a decade), recite a Hail Mary while reflecting on the mystery.

❖ On the next large bead, recite the Glory Be.

❖ The FATIMA PRAYER may be said here:

"OH MY JESUS, forgive us our sins, save us from the fires of hell, lead all souls to heaven, especially those in most need of Thy mercy.

❖ Begin the next decade by recalling the next mystery and reciting an Our Father. Move to the small beads and pray 10 Hail Marys while meditating on the mystery.

❖ Continue until you have circled the entire Rosary (five decades), or for a full Rosary you will circle it four times (twenty decades).

❖ It is customary to CONCLUDE with the following prayers:

HAIL HOLY QUEEN

"HAIL, HOLY QUEEN, mother of mercy, our life, our sweetness, and our hope. To thee do we cry, poor banished children of Eve. To thee do we send up our sighs, mourning and weeping in this valley of tears. Turn then, most gracious advocate, thine eyes of mercy toward us, and after this our exile, show us the blessed fruit of thy womb, Jesus. O clement, O loving, O sweet Virgin Mary.

(Verse) Pray for us, O Holy Mother of God.

(Response) That we may be made worthy of the promises of Christ."

ROSARY PRAYER

(Verse) Let us pray,

(Response) O God, whose only begotten Son, by His life, death and resurrection, has purchased for us the rewards of eternal salvation, grant we beseech Thee, that while meditating on these mysteries of the most Holy Rosary of the Blessed Virgin Mary, we may imitate what they contain and obtain what they promise, through Christ our Lord. Amen.

Most Sacred Heart of Jesus, have mercy on us.

Immaculate Heart of Mary, pray for us.

In the Name of the Father, and of the Son, and of the Holy Spirit. Amen.

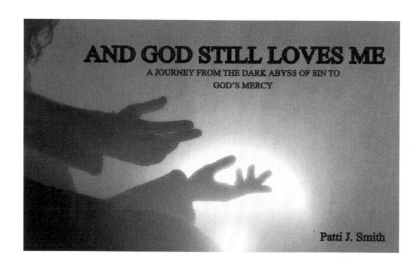

AND GOD STILL LOVES ME

A JOURNEY FROM THE DARK ABYSS OF SIN TO
GOD'S MERCY

Patti J. Smith

SINNER

Jesus, I have failed you
by all my words and deeds.
I walked the path of faithlessness,
to meet my selfish needs.

I hurt all those around me,
without a second thought
of all the damage I had caused
and all the pain I brought.

I placed myself in that abyss,
encased in Satan's shroud.
But your hand reached in to pull me up,
and from that time I vowed.

That I would share with everyone
despite my life of sin.
You graciously still loved me,
and let me live again.

Table of Contents

Foreword

"All have sinned and have fallen short of the glory of God"

Romans 3:23

This is a story of a sinner, like you and I, who has fallen short but through God's love, grace and mercy has come around to know God's glory.

Patti attended a Rachel's Hope After Abortion Healing Retreat, which I was leading, in May, 2009. Her story was one filled with much dysfunction, bad choices and tears of regrets. Yet even during these times the hand of God was there preserving her life.

She has since volunteered to co-lead several Rachel's Hope retreats. Because of her past experiences and her spiritual growth she has the ability to relate to the women and direct them in a heartfelt, compassionate and understanding way. She has also co-led a retreat at the Las Colinas Women's Jail where she was also able to be a role model for the women who have been involved in drug and alcohol abuse, as most of the women in the jail are there with drug related charges.

The article following her story, "Turning Your Lifelong Regrets into Immeasurable Graces" was written by my late husband, Jim Benefield. It sums up where her journey has taken her. It has taken her into repentance, forgiveness, healing and appreciation for what God has brought up out of her darkness. She is able to move forward with grace to help others who have made

some of the same choices she made in her life. Scripture further exemplifies these graces in Romans 8:28 "All things work together for good for those who love God and are called according to His purpose."

Rosemary Benefield RN, MA, MPC
Executive Director
Rachel's Hope After Abortion Healing Retreats

Introduction

There are so many people who want to turn back the hands of time and have a "do-over", and I used to be one of them. I wanted a new life, I wanted to forget, I wanted to erase the pain inflicted on my family, friends and myself, but most of all I wanted to die. This book is about a lost soul who shunned God and hurt everyone in her path.

One would expect my journey was a result of a terrible childhood or lack of opportunities. That's definitely not the case. I was a military brat and had a wonderful life. My parents were loving and supportive and set an example of how to live a Christian life. We were a close family who always ate meals together, played board games in the evenings and had many road adventures. As a child I was involved in Brownies, Girl Scouts and Job's Daughters, in fact, I am a Past Honored Queen. In my adult life I worked for the government for fifteen years, starting out as a typist and ending my career as an auditor for an Inspector General's office; I served ten years in the Army Reserve reaching the rank of Staff Sergeant; I worked as a school secretary/office manager for ten years; I was a union president. Sounds like I had it all together, doesn't it? Nothing could be further from the truth. My descent began right after high school and continued to spiral downward for the next twenty-six years.

My abuse of alcohol played an integral part of who I was; however, it would be hypocritical to use it as justification. I chose to drink and I am responsible for all of my actions, no matter how reprehensible.

Revisiting the demons of my past not only dredged up immeasurable pain, sorrow and shame, it uncovered more. I was tempted many times to stop writing because I was fearful of what else would surface, but God put me on this mission and I put my trust in Him.

To reveal all my demons would involve years of writing and this book would be longer than War and Peace; therefore, I chose to share certain events or situations I felt altered my life and best exemplified how deeply I went into the black abyss of godlessness. There are a few events in this book that have never been discussed with my parents, family or friends; however, it's time to let it all go. I pray they understand my purpose and are not hurt, embarrassed or feel betrayed.

I'm not proud of my past, but pray my story will give renewed hope to those walking or who have walked the same path. They need to know there is light at the top of that abyss, and that light is God's merciful and unfailing love.

Author's Note: In order to protect privacy, * by a name will indicate a pseudonym.

Chapter 1
The Price Of Promiscuity

"Let us conduct ourselves becomingly as in the day, not in reveling and drunkenness, not in debauchery and licentiousness, not in quarreling and jealousy."

Romans 13:13

I wasn't really popular in high school because I felt everyone was better than me. The few friends I had were prettier, slimmer, had long hair, good grades and most importantly, self-confidence. I was afraid to voice my opinion, and just followed the crowd. I didn't try anything unless someone else did it before me. I was a coward. The latter part of my senior year I started to bloom with a little help from a "friend", alcohol. I didn't drink that much at first, but when I turned twenty-one, everything changed. This wallflower turned into a welcomed part of the bar scene. Once drunk, I was <u>somebody</u>! I actually felt attractive and because of my new found confidence was actively pursued by men. I was very naive and didn't realize I was being used. I had a nickname back then which was not cute, nor attractive: "Pass around Patti", but I earned it. I went through men as quickly as I did bottles of booze.

I had a penchant for band members so I would go to bars early, grab the table closest to the stage and start drinking. I would always dress in provocative outfits, dance seductively, and use all types of body language to get their attention. I'm embarrassed just thinking about it. Most times it worked and I ended up taking a band member home or end up in his hotel room. Eventually my reputation preceded me and they would know what to expect and I didn't let them down. Through the years I became less and less selective. There were so many mornings when I woke up next to a total stranger wondering who he was, where I was and how I got there. To further exemplify, when I lived in Seattle a big event was Sea Fair which brought in many Navy ships. Since my favorite bar was on the waterfront it was full of eager sailors looking for a good time. As with my band members, I didn't disappoint them. I had no fear for my safety in those days and would take any one of them home after they bought me a few drinks then take them back to the ship. This cycle continued throughout Fleet Week and embarrassingly enough, I never took the same sailor home twice..... So many sailors so little time.

My favorite bar was conveniently owned by a close friend of mine and was not only on the waterfront but close to my office. I would go directly there after work where a drink was waiting for me. When I walked in, men's eyebrows would raise and they would look at each other. They knew the drill and knew that one of them would be my next target. A co-worker of mine once made a snide remark about my reputation and I was very insulted. I accused him of being jealous and informed him I was very desirable and everyone wanted me. To prove that point I got up from the table, located the nearest man sitting alone and started my routine. I then took him across the street to the building where I worked and had relations with him on the floor of my boss's office. We returned to the bar and bragged to my co-worker. I thought he would be impressed but he just stared at me in disbelief and I'm sure with total disgust and pity.

Then there was my "modeling". Once a month my friend would have a local lingerie designer come in to the bar to show the newest creations. After I got a few under my belt, I would grab the slinkiest negligee available, go to the ladies room, take off my street clothes and put it on. I would then saunter back into the bar, parade around and lean seductively over tables. Not only did I have my choice of men, I got a great discount on what I modeled. Looking back, I'm sure the discount was to ensure I purchased the items I wore. Who would want to buy something that intimate worn by someone like me?

My behavior put me in so many dangerous situations I'm lucky I came out alive, in fact, I used to party at a seedy establishment near the Seattle Airport where the Green River Killer used to go and it was during the time he was active. His sights were set on prostitutes and I could have very easily been one of his victims. I wasn't a prostitute per se, but my behavior definitely leaned towards that direction. Alcohol gave me a sense of being indestructible but in all actuality, I was obviously vulnerable. I know now God had other plans for me, otherwise my photo would be side by side with other murder victims on a police department bulletin board.

Revealing this part of my life is hard and admitting the level of my promiscuity is excruciating; however, I feel it's necessary to be brutally honest. I've been with, to the best of my recollection, around 90 men.

What is more disgusting and humiliating is 90 is probably low because I had so many alcoholic black-outs.

My promiscuity was not void of consequences. I didn't escape disease but fortunately I didn't contract anything incurable, and I didn't escape pregnancy which will be addressed later. But there was that night...

A bouncer asked me to meet him after the bar closed. Of course, I agreed. He was good looking and I had been eying him for quite some time. I was watching a friend's house so I told him to meet me there. Unbeknownst to me, he was not alone. All I remember is being on a red metal kitchen table and having them take turns. I couldn't distinguish one face from the other; I felt detached. After it was over and they left, I just sat there dazed. Did I report it? No. Did I tell anyone? No. I thought I deserved it and pushed it back into the deepest part of my mind and sadly, continued going to that bar as if nothing had happened.

Although the gang rape was bad enough, I think the most damaging consequence of my whoring around was the demise of my desire for intimacy. After the first dozen men or so, I didn't enjoy sex, but I was really good at faking it. In actuality, I prostituted myself, not for money, but for what I thought was acceptance, attention and love.

Luke 7:36-50 speaks of an immoral woman, a new believer, who upon hearing Jesus was at the Pharisee's house, found her way in. She was ashamed of who she was and wouldn't even look him in the eye or speak but washed his feet with her tears and dried them with her hair, the only way she could think of to honor him. He lifts up her face tells her, "Your faith has saved you; go in peace." Jesus knew she was repentant and forgave her without her even asking. He knew her heart, just as he knows mine.

Coming to the point of being freed from my promiscuous past is a work in progress. I accepted responsibility, repented and was forgiven. I sometimes stumble back into the guilt and shame, but those times are slowly diminishing. I know in the deepest recesses of my heart that God has forgiven me and through His mercy I have also been able to forgive myself.

Chapter 2
Women Beware

"For the lips of an adulteress drip honey, and her speech is smoother than oil; but in the end she is bitter as wormwood, sharp as a two-edged sword. Her feet go down to death; her steps follow the path to Sheol". She does not take heed to the path of life; her ways wander, and she does not know it. And now, O sons, listen to me, and do not depart from the words of my mouth."

Proverbs 5:3

With all the men I had in my life, I hate to admit, the majority were either married or in long-term relationships. I also hate to admit that one of those "conquests" was after I sobered up. The affairs were mostly short-lived. There were a few one-night stands, one of which was a husband of a friend that was in alcohol rehabilitation and one was a husband of a co-worker that was in the hospital for surgery. I had one affair with a boyfriend of a co-worker which was quite a challenge. She, her boyfriend and I were on the same bowling league and we partied together all the time. Some mornings she would come to work and tell me he hadn't been home the night before and was wondering if he was seeing someone else. Of course, those nights in question he was spending with me and I would look her straight in the eye, chuckle and tell her she was just being paranoid.

I convinced myself that being with a married or committed man would keep me from getting hurt. I felt I had more control and felt I had accomplished some great feat by bedding another woman's man. The truth is I had no control at all and it definitely was not something to be considered an accomplishment. The long-term affairs resulted in me spending most of my time waiting for them to call or for a night they could get away. And of course, I always spent holidays alone.   It was a miserable existence but I convinced myself it was worth it...until I fell in love.

At the time I was in the Army Reserve and those two weeks of active duty each year was a "field of dreams" for me.   I would select my prey months before we left for our duty location. One of those affairs started before our annual training and carried over after our return. I went into this one like all the others, non-committed, just a fling, but for some reason I let my guard down and fell head over heels in love. *Bill did too, so I thought. You've heard the stories when a man will tell a woman he loves her and that he's going to leave his wife. I would say the majority of the time it's a lie to keep the affair going but I thought my situation was different. I kept hearing that promise over and over again with no action. He said he was waiting for the "right time", wanted to get his finances in order, etc., etc., etc., Always an excuse. Well, being the patient person I was, I decided to help him along. He had a convention out of town and he invited me to come along. To me this was the perfect time to get things settled once and for all. I conspired with a friend of mine that after Bill and I had arrived at our destination, a call would be made to his wife informing her he had another woman with him. I figured that would be it, she would get angry, kick him out and he'd be mine forever. Well, as they say, the best made plans.....

Sometime around three in the morning someone was banging on our hotel room door. In a post-drunken stupor, I went to the door and asked who it was and the voice said she had an emergency message for me about my parents. Of course, not thinking why I wasn't notified by phone, I opened the door. There stood the wife, shoving her way into the room. I was mortified. Bill heard his wife's voice, sat up with eyes as big as saucers. She, by then, was sitting on the dresser opposite the bed. Having answered the door undressed, (I know this sounds comical) I crawled back into the bed and covered up. What a sight this must have been. She just sat there staring at us for what seemed like hours. I had no idea what to say or do. She finally looked at me and asked me if her husband said he loved me and was going to leave her, and I said yes. She looked at him and asked if what I said was true and he told her no. My heart sank. He got up, got dressed and left with her. My whole world collapsed. I was totally humiliated. Not once did I blame myself for setting this up and forcing the issue, I blamed him. He was the liar and I was the victim. How heartless could I have been? Me, the victim? What about his wife? That poor woman not only heard about her husband's infidelity, she witnessed it first-hand. She was the one humiliated and devastated, but in my self-centered mind she had nothing to do with the equation at all. I was one wicked witch that wanted something, regardless of the cost.

You would think that after that experience I would have learned a lesson, but I didn't. I continued to have affairs; however, I didn't set up any more confrontations. I allowed myself to be used, pretending to be loved. I never realized that every time I entered into that type of relationship, a little more of me died inside.

HAPPY, BUT NOT PROUD

This next story is how my current marriage started. I'm not proud of the circumstances and there is no justification for it, but I promised myself to be honest.

After I sobered up and started going to AA meetings, I met a really nice man who had wonderful heart and soul. We would go out for coffee with other people after meetings and talk for hours. Well, that friendship grew into romance. This time it was not intentional. I had recently separated from my second husband and filed for divorce. I wasn't looking for a relationship at all and Mike was married. We both knew it was wrong but continued anyway. He was in an unhappy marriage and had considered leaving his wife several times but he hadn't because of his daughter. As time went on he decided to leave her and he moved in with me. Obviously, his wife was angry and hurt and his daughter was most understandably disappointed in her father. Both blamed me for the break-up. There was quite a bit of stress in our relationship and I know it was because how it began; but this time was extraordinarily different because there was love on both sides. You would think that would be the end of it and we lived happily ever, but that's not the way it happened. Mike woke up one morning and with tears in his eyes he told me he had to go "home". He missed his daughter and wanted to see if he could salvage his marriage. Again, I was crushed but this time I didn't feel like the victim. I knew deep down in my heart he was right but it didn't take the hurt away. I came very close to drinking again and I had been sober for almost two years. Mike moved home and started marriage counseling with his wife. He tried to mend the fences with his daughter. During that time I was totally lost, bereft of spirit and empty. I admit I drove by his house a lot and hoped to see him at AA meetings but he was avoiding me. I wanted to see him and try to make sense of what had happened and find out what I had done wrong (other than fall in love with a married man). I was inconsolable. Yes, this was different than how I was before. I didn't shrug it off and move on. I finally asked a friend if she could contact him for me to set up a time we could talk. Mike reluctantly agreed and met me after an AA meeting. We sat on the tailgate of his truck and he told me things weren't any better in his marriage but he was still trying. I wanted to beg him to come back but I didn't. I just cried and told him how much I missed him but I understood what he was saying. We both went our separate ways and when I got home the phone rang. It was Mike. His wife had asked someone to follow him to that meeting. Now don't get me wrong, I'm not blaming her, she had every right to not trust him, it's just sad she didn't know what Mike was telling me. Anyway, when he went home that night, his bags were packed. He moved back in with me and we have been together now for fourteen years.

It's not to say things have always been rosy. At the beginning, we had to deal with a strained relationship with his daughter along with disappointment and disapproval from friends and family. We worked through those trials together and little by little our friends and family started to see this was not just a fling. Mike's relationship with his daughter has improved and they spend time together; unfortunately, she still has issues with me. She is a beautiful, funny, intelligent young woman and I would love to have her be a large part in both of our lives, but I can't expect her to love me, or even feel close to me. I can't expect her to want a relationship with my parents or my side of the family. That is my penance for entering into a relationship with her dad before his marriage had ended.

Although my marriage is strong, I would not recommend a relationship starting that way. I have to be honest about my lack of trust. The first years of our marriage I was terribly insecure. I was thinking, "What if I do something wrong, will he have an affair, or go back to his ex-wife?" My friends would warn me that if he did it once he would do it again and repeat that old adage "a leopard never changes his spots".

Fortunately, nothing like that ever occurred and my insecurities are gone. He has always been open and honest with me and, although we have had our share of disagreements and challenges, we work through them together and our love continues to grow.

Chapter 3
Sins Of The Daughter

"If one curses his father or his mother,
his lamp will be put out in utter darkness. "

Proverbs 20:20

My mom and dad are truly wonderful people and caring and dedicated parents. All of my antics caused them a great deal of embarrassment and hurt. My mom is a very prim and proper lady and was raised old school where you saved yourself for marriage, wore respectable clothing, etc. I used to tease her because my sister was born nine months and one day after the day she and my dad married. I would say, "Hey Mom, was Diane late or early?" She would blush and get really flustered.. My dad was a little more laid back but being in the military, he ran a tight ship, had very high morals and specific expectations of behavior. My sister and I were both raised in the same household with the same rules, etc., however, she was more compliant and I ended up the renegade.

My mom and dad were not only exposed to my promiscuity via gossip, which was rampant in our small town, but they witnessed it as well. I would come home drunk with my hair all messed up, covered in hickeys with not a care in the world. They tried their best to control me when I lived at home and although I ignored their demands, they never kicked me out. I remember one time in particular, I had come home drunk and my mom was sitting at the kitchen table. She asked where I had been and what I had been doing and I told her to f—off. The shock and hurt in her face as well as my dad's is a vision that is as clear today as it was when it happened over 30 years ago. When I moved to Seattle I think they were relieved because at least they would have a little peace, but not for long...

*Jim, my second husband (my first will be addressed later) and was a friend of my mom and dad's. He lived in Southern California but met my folks through family that lived in my home town. I met him one weekend when I traveled from Seattle to visit my folks. His aunt had passed away and had some business to take care of so my folks asked him to stay at their house. A few months later, he was trying to reach them to chat but couldn't, so he called me to see where they were. We talked for quite awhile and during that conversation he invited me to Southern California for a weekend. Being footloose and fancy-free, and remembering he liked to party, I took him up on it. I didn't tell my parents where I was going because my dad's mom had passed away and they wanted me to go with them to Central California for the funeral. I told them I had to work. So while my mom and dad were mourning the death of my grandmother, I was partying like crazy only a five-hour drive away. What a wretched, selfish daughter I was. Two days after I returned to Seattle, Jim called me at my local bar and proposed. He flew up to Seattle two weeks later and we got married at the courthouse with my friend (and bartender) as my maid of honor. None of my family knew what was happening. He called my mom and dad after the ceremony, from a bar, to tell them he had gotten married. They were happy for him and asked if it was anyone they knew…well, you can imagine their reaction when he told them. We went to see them a few days later and told them about how this came about. I was so stupid to not realize they could put two and two together and figure out I lied about why I had to miss my grandmother's funeral. Both of them were crushed, especially my dad, but at that point I didn't care. I found a husband and drinking buddy all in one. Without a second thought, I abruptly quit my job, packed up and was on my way to Southern California with a man I barely knew.

To this day I don't know why they just didn't wash their hands of me all together. I allowed them to take the blame for a lot of what happened, but it wasn't their fault. My actions were my choice. I didn't care who I hurt, I just wanted to do what I wanted and have fun. The more miserable everyone else was, I seemed to be happier. I have spent the last fifteen years making amends to them and I thank God their hearts remained open.

My relationship with my parents reminds me of the Story of the Prodigal Son (Luke 15:11 – 32). In that story, a man had two sons and one of them asked for his inheritance early and left the family home. He wasted his inheritance on wild behavior and before long he was broke. He tried to remain on his own but realized he could not. In humility he returns home and his father welcomed him back with open arms and lavished him with a banquet fit for a king. The other son could not understand his father's behavior because he was the "good one" and did what he was expected to do. The father told his angry son he has always been there and still has his fortune and he too should be glad because his brother is no longer lost to sin.

My parents didn't throw a big banquet for me when I found my way back to Christ, it took them awhile to realize it was real. My actions spoke louder than words. They are in their mid-80's and just recently moved in with my husband and me. Never in my wildest dreams would I have imagined they would trust me enough to take care of them in their golden years. God has given me that wonderful opportunity and I will not take one moment for granted. We have talked about the past and have even had a few chuckles, but what really brings tears to my eyes is that they are finally proud of me.

Chapter 4
Unfortunate Marriage

"Wives, be subject to your husbands, as is fitting in the Lord."
Colossians 3:12-19

On the drive to my new home in Southern California after Jim and I married, I had a sick feeling in my stomach. I pushed that feeling aside and convinced myself I was happy. Why wouldn't I be? He loved to drink, he had money in the bank and had just purchased four acres in a small town, where no one knew my history. I could reinvent myself!

The first few months of our marriage were pretty good. I met his family and friends and we started building a ranch, accumulating horses, goats, chickens, etc. Between getting the ranch together and drinking continuously, the days all melded together. I kept getting that sick feeling in my stomach but ignored it. I should have known something was wrong when he would send me to the store, which was eighteen miles away, and I would want him to come with me every time. I was afraid if I got in that car alone, I would just keep driving. Once we got everything together on the ranch, we had drained most of our funds so we both started working. Having the opportunity to be sober and away from him for eight hours shed light on how unhappy I was. I had feigned enjoyment at being a homemaker and wife and I tried to convince myself and others things were wonderful.

Jim had a really dry, cutting wit and was also very intelligent. I too had a cutting wit and intelligence; however, he never considered me his equal. If we ever got into a deep conversation about a particular subject and I voiced my opinion, he demeaned me. He would say I didn't have a clue what I was talking about. There were occasions where comments were made in front of other people. This was not only embarrassing, but started a rapid disintegration of my self-esteem and self-worth. Although I couldn't compete with his demeaning comments, I was very talented at pushing his buttons. I would tell him his drinking and attitude caused his kids from not visiting more, his job menial labor, and constantly reminded him my job was much more prestigious. I would go on and on about how I expected more from him that he should remember I left a career and all of my friends in Seattle, just for him. In retrospect, I think we were both losing our self-esteem and self-worth and destroying each other was our way of maintaining some sense of pride.

As mentioned earlier, I had issues with intimacy but as long as I was drunk I could convince anyone, including myself, I was enjoying it. I was able to maintain the façade for a year and a half into the marriage then couldn't hide it any longer. I started making excuses or started a fight to give me a reason to sleep in the spare room or on the couch. Of course, this infuriated Jim, but I didn't care. His frustrations grew and he used to warn me that I had better become a real wife, or else. I didn't know what "or else" was, but I told him if he didn't like it, please feel free to go elsewhere for relief. The first time I said those words I could see the hurt in his eyes. Regardless of how bad our marriage was, he never once strayed.

Because of the never ending flow of booze in the household, my intimacy issues would be a focal point. One night, Jim's frustration was more than he could handle. He put something in my beer and forced himself on me. I didn't know what was happening and I was powerless. I was always fearful after that, but it never happened again. I think he was remorseful that he stooped to that level and to be honest, although it was a humiliating and frightening experience, I didn't blame him. I had entered into a marriage that should never had happened and lived a lie that destroyed us both. Instead of accepting the truth, we both just continued to drink and be miserable until I hit bottom.

We separated after I reached a year of sobriety and ten years of marriage. Believe it or not, it was a hard decision. Although I was miserable, it was the only life I knew and the thought of being alone again was frightening. Jim was surprised when I approached him about the separation and when he moved his things out of the house he cried. The tears broke my heart as I realized at that moment that he must have really loved me despite everything. I started to reconsider; however, continued with the separation and subsequent divorce, not out of hate or anger, but out of self-preservation. Because he had not stopped drinking, the temptation was there. I am certain I would have eventually lost my resolve and relapsed right back into that drunken nightmare.

Jim never sobered up and passed away in 2011. Although we never had a true marriage, I think I loved him in my own way and regret never making amends to him. No matter how bad our marriage was, it takes two and I was definitely not the victim.

I firmly believe that sick feeling it the pit of my stomach was God's way of telling me this was not the right man for me. Instead of listening to Him, I did what I always did ... exactly what I wanted to do, regardless of the consequences. In Psalms 81:11-14, it says, "I am the LORD your God, who brought you up from the land of Egypt. Open wide your mouth that I may fill it. But my people did not listen to my words; Israel would not submit to me. So I thrust them away to the hardness of their heart; Let them walk in their own machinations. O that my people would listen to me, that Israel would walk in my ways. In a moment I would humble their foes and turn back my hand against their oppressors".

I now live by those verses as best I can. Whenever a decision needs to be made I try to stay quiet and listen to God. If something doesn't "feel right", I try set aside free-will and go with God. I'm not always successful at listening but I'm blessed to not suffer the dire consequences as I did before. I now know all I need to do is humbly ask God to forgive me for my failings. I can then pick myself up and try again.

Chapter 5
Bless The Children

"Fathers, do not provoke your children,
lest they become discouraged."

Colossians 3:21

Jim had two children from a previous marriage who lived with his ex-wife. They too were surprised when he married me, as they never knew I existed, which in actuality, I hadn't. On the drive down to Southern California I fantasized about how wonderful it was going to be, having a built-in family. I knew I was going to be a wonderful step-mother. I tried so very hard to get them to like me but it never happened and my insecurities began to surface. I drank all the time during their visits to assuage the fear I had in failing and they took advantage of my drunkenness. What normal kid wouldn't? They would talk back, tease me, play cruel tricks (like putting Windex in my beer); anything to get a reaction. That reaction, of course, was not parental by any means. I would throw tearful temper tantrums and use every expletive in the world. I know that behavior scared them a great deal and poor Jim didn't know what to do. He really loved his boys and knew my behavior created their reluctance to visit. He did try to limit both of our drinking when they were with us; however, that exacerbated my explosiveness. The other thing that infuriated me was the boys reminding me I wasn't their mother and they didn't have to do anything I said. I was compared to her on so many occasions, my insecurity turned into rage and there's nothing worse than an angry drunk. It resulted in my dark obsession with destroying HER. I would run her down in front of the boys. I started coercing Jim to try to get more visitation, attempt to obtain full custody, etc. I didn't want those boys living with us, they hated me. I just wanted to hurt her because I didn't measure up.

A couple of years into our marriage we adopted a ten-year old, Bobby, out of foster care. To this day I am totally convinced we should have received an Academy Award for acting. During all the background checks and surprise home visits from social workers, no one ever realized we were drunks. Bobby was a student at the elementary school where I was working at the time. The county was trying to find a permanent home for him and we decided why not us? I thought having a child of my own would help alleviate my insecurities that had been evolving due to my step-sons and secretly hoped it would strengthen my marriage. Don't get me wrong, I fell in love with Bobby the minute I saw him in the principal's office. He was emotionally needy, injured and angry and I think now … we were kindred spirits.

Obviously, when you adopt an older child that has been in the system as long as he had, there are going to be adjustment and emotional issues. Being a true alcoholic, I figured I could handle anything and I could fix him. That was definitely not the case. The more he misbehaved the more I drank. I'm not blaming Bobby for any of my bad choices as it was all me. My behavior towards him was very similar to my step-sons, but I think he suffered more because he was there all the time. He never knew what to expect emotionally from me, a high or a low. He never knew how I would react to any given situation. Sometimes I would be all loving and forgiving and other times I would demean him unmercifully. Not too long ago, he reminded me of an incident that he had never forgotten. We were making chocolate chip cookies and I asked him to mix the batter. He was a perfectionist and wanted so much to please me. He kept stirring and stirring until all the chocolate chips melted. I got so angry I took the cookie batter and dumped it on his head. Not only did this frighten him, he still stays out of the kitchen when I'm baking. Needless to say, my actions most definitely created more problems for him. He ended up being institutionalized as he became a threat to himself and others. The guilt I felt when we left him at the facility was overwhelming. I know now he had more issues then Jim and I could deal with, but I also know the atmosphere that poor child was adopted into was a contributing factor. My feelings of inadequacy were insurmountable at that point which started the beginning of my final descent.

The treatment my son received was successful and he eventually returned home. He's a grown man now and has children of his own.

Despite his miserable childhood, he is a wonderful, loving father. One of his daughters is autistic and he is patient, compassionate and loving. I love him dearly and am very proud of him and I hope he's finally proud of me.

In regards to my step-sons, I regret never establishing a true loving relationship with them. After Jim and I divorced there was no more contact. They have moved on in their lives and I don't expect them to change their opinion of me; however, my son is still in contact with them and he has shared I'm not the same person anymore. They do know I am repentant for my actions and I pray their hearts, as well as their mother's, are open to forgiveness.

Chapter 6
Cursing God

"And the tongue is a fire. The tongue is an unrighteous world among our members, staining the whole body, setting on fire the cycle of nature, and set on fire by hell."

James 3:6

I can't count the times I cursed God and I can imagine Him with a pad of paper tallying the times I did. It was so easy to look at Him and assign blame for minor issues such as a car breaking down; however, when someone dies, that's a totally different story. There were four significant losses that truly brought me to the breaking point.

The first was the murder of my friend's three and a half year old daughter. *Ann was one of my closest friends in high school and when she and her husband, *Carl were married, I was her maid of honor. When their daughter was born it was a wonderful moment. They both loved her very much and she was a happy, beautiful child. Ann had gone to work one day and Carl was home with their daughter. Something happened and he snapped. He took an iron and beat that beautiful child to death. This was entirely unexpected as there had been no prior abusive incidents. He was a nice guy who loved his wife and daughter dearly. It was determined he had some sort of psychotic break.

There were two pictures in my mind that haunted me for years; one was that of walking into the chapel and seeing that little pink casket that held an innocent child who had such a wonderful life ahead of her, and the other was of that precious child looking up at her daddy and asking, "Why?" I was immersed in grief...I felt sorry for myself. Because of my alcoholic self-centeredness, I could not offer any consolation to my friend or her family. Their devastation was immeasurable compared to mine but I was incapable of seeing it. I could not understand why God would allow something this horrendous to happen, and was angry I was not given the compassion to be there for them.

Ann and I became estranged a few years after the tragedy, primarily due to the same alcoholic self-centeredness and insensitivity. We never reestablished the close relationship we had so many years prior for which I take full responsibility. Although she never remarried or had other children, she was able to move forward and become quite successful.

Carl pleaded insanity and was committed to a mental hospital; however, was eventually released. Through research I found out he continued to have problems after his release. Based on how much he loved his daughter and wife, I'm sure the guilt overwhelmed him, regardless of the treatment he received. According to public records, he had been placed under conservatorship in another state and died a few years ago. It wouldn't surprise me if it was due to suicide.

Another friend, *Sue, and I were also high school friends and shared the joys of that time…high school crushes, skipping school and sleepovers. She took the whole back page of my senior yearbook, reminding me of all the fun times and at the end she said, "I'll never forget you as long as I live." Who knew she would be gone just a few years after writing that.

She married a man she met at college and I was honored to be a bridesmaid. After about a year, her marriage disintegrated and she moved back in with her parents. It was then she was diagnosed with kidney failure and needed a transplant. She and her family still lived in our small home-town, where there were no specialized medical facilities. In order for her to get the best treatment, her family relocated to a larger city. By that time I had been transferred and promoted to the opposite side of the state. I visited from time to time but those visits were few and far between. When I was there, I didn't spend much time with her. I was more interested in drinking and finding a guy to hang out with. Sue died at the age of twenty-three due to the rejection of her transplant. When her mother called to inform me of her death I was heartbroken and cursed God. I blamed Him for her death and was angry He didn't compel me to focus on her instead of myself. I was convinced He took away my chance to say good-by and show her how much I loved her. She had always been a true friend to me and here I was, using her as an excuse to party and fool around.

Even in death I let her down. I contacted her ex-husband to let him know about her passing and promptly began a relationship with him. In fact, he was one of the possible fathers of my first aborted child. How mortified her family, or mine for that matter, would have been had they known. Again, my desires came first.

Gayle's parents were my mom and dad's best friends. They met in England and almost delivered me in the back seat of a car on the way to the hospital. Our families stayed close even though the military sent us different directions. They retired in Oregon and when I relocated to Seattle, Gayle and I would visit each other quite a bit. We would stay up for hours laughing and joking. My favorite memory was when we decided to meet our vacationing parents in Reno. When they met our plane, much to their embarrassment, we staggered down the steps in drunken laughter. That whole trip was full of laughter and high jinks. My uncle had gotten married that weekend and was on his honeymoon. We made sure the "early maid service" door tag was put up on their door. We also would take the tips our parents left on restaurant tables and use them to play Keno. She knew all of my secrets and kept them (including the butterfly tattoo she convinced me to get). She was the only person I actually listened to. She held nothing back and was brutally honest towards my lifestyle but she loved me and was always there when I needed her. Again, it was a one-way street. If I had something better to do I would ignore her calls and make excuses for not visiting. I loved her and respected her but again, my priorities were elsewhere. After I married my Jim and moved to California we would talk occasionally on the phone and I would always promise to visit. One day the phone rang and it was her dad informing me she died. She had a heart attack at forty-seven. In my eyes God failed me again. He allowed me to make the same mistake as I had with Sue.

I met Laurie in AA. I remember her walking up to me after a meeting one night saying, "Hi, my name is Laurie, will you be my friend?" I was taken aback by that question but she was sincere and we indeed became friends. She was struggling with her sobriety, having relapsed after twelve years, but was resolute in her desire to get right back into the program. She also suffered from depression, as did I, so we could definitely relate to one another. We would get together for dinners with our husbands, who would just shake their heads at us as we talked non-stop about everything under the sun. One night she called me and was extremely happy. We again had a very long conversation...then realized it was time to hang up. We said our good-byes with an "I Love You". The next day she went into the garage, took a gun to her head and pulled the trigger. She left a husband, a seven year old son and a five year old daughter. Although I was getting my spiritual house in order, I once again cursed God for allowing this to happen. Her husband and children were inconsolable and were trying to make sense of it. All I could think of was why didn't she say anything to me? Did she say something that I didn't hear? Why didn't God give me some sort of message as to what she was thinking so I could have stopped her?

4 James 1:17 "Every good endowment and every perfect gift is from above, coming down from the Father of lights with whom there is no variation or shadow due to change."

Cursing God is one way to betray Him but looking back, taking Him for granted is another. We see His work every day and do we thank Him? We see beautiful landscape and chalk it up to great weather. We get a great job and praise ourselves. We survive an illness or accident and call it luck. I realized through this journey of mine that nothing in this world would be, if not for God. All beauty we see or experience is through His love and mercy.

I was sickly as a child and back in the fifties they could not diagnose what was wrong; in fact, my parents were told I was not going to survive. Until age twelve I suffered from cyclic vomiting, dizziness and I was extremely tiny. There were other maladies along the way, of which one was an allergy to my own hair which resulted in a rash all over my body. A very astute dermatologist just happened to review my medical history and sent me for a chest x-ray after he heard a little murmur in my heart. Before I knew it I was scheduled for open heart surgery. All my illnesses from birth to then were due to a quarter-sized hole in my heart. Because of my weakened state and the fact that type of surgery was still relatively new, I was given a forty percent survival chance at the time of surgery. Needless to say I survived and thrived.

When I was about twenty-three I had gone to my hometown to visit my parents and get baptized with my sister in a Methodist Church. I could have cared less about the baptism but decided it would appease my parents and maybe put me in a better light. I also wanted to visit my favorite haunts and party with old friends. The baptism never happened. I was invited to an intramural baseball game and I decided that was a perfect way to while away the time until the bars opened up. The batter lost grip of the bat and it ended up flying into the bleachers onto my forehead. I ended up with multiple skull fractures, a subdural hematoma, a concussion and 28 stitches. The doctors prepared my parents for the worst. When my mom was in the emergency room watching me get stitched up I remember telling her, "See Mom, even God doesn't want me".

These events were indeed miracles and I never acknowledged it was God. When I was hit with the bat, God <u>did</u> want me and he wanted me alive. He has saved me so many other times as well and I know the way to show my gratitude is to walk with Him, share His word and be open to His will.

Chapter 7

Take and Violate

"The integrity of the upright guides them,
but the crookedness of the treacherous destroys them."

Proverbs 11:3

When we visualize theft, we see a masked person robbing a bank or a store, breaking into a home or stealing a car. Well, that is true. However, there are other ways to steal as well. During my demon years I stole a great deal. I stole trust.

There were many people in my life that counted on me; my parents, sister, husbands, child, friends, employers and co-workers. In previous chapters you read about how I failed my parents, my son and friends. I took all the trust they gave me knowing full well I was going to violate it.

My sister was not immune to my offenses. She trusted me as any sister would, even enough to watch her children. This is a perfect example of my mind-set: She and her husband were delayed getting home once and I had a man to meet so I did what I always did … what I wanted...and left my young nieces and nephew alone. She was furious that I put her children in harm's way but I turned it around and accused her of being inconsiderate by expecting me to wait for their return. She had also trusted me to set an example to her children and what did I do? I was staying overnight at her house one night and she had fixed me up with a friend of hers. I ended up staying at his place and coming home the next day, crumpled clothes and all. She voiced her disapproval and following my usual pattern, blamed her because she set it up. My theft of her trust continued for many, many years under a variety of circumstances. I know and understand that, although I have changed, it would take a great deal of time to redeem myself. Unfortunately, her heart was not open to forgiveness and my many attempts to reconcile were met with judgment and reliving the past. We are estranged to this day which saddens me and my parents considerably.

As indicated earlier, I have been married three times. I've discussed the second and third husbands; however, I'll now address the first. *Mark and I were best friends in elementary school and although our parents were in the military and relocated, we kept in touch. When he graduated from high school he went into the Army. After basic training he came to visit and we got engaged. A few months later I broke it off because I was in college and didn't want to be tied down. There weren't any real fireworks over it and I went on with my life. About ten years later he looked me up and invited me to visit him in Colorado for New Year's. As with my second husband, I was footloose and fancy-free so decided to take him up on it. We partied a lot and had a great time. He ended up quitting college, packing up and moving up to Seattle in February and in March we got married. I knew while walking down the aisle it wasn't right but I did it anyway. My parents warned me, I did it anyway. My friends warned me, I did it anyway. There was nothing wrong with him, he was a really nice guy, I just wasn't in love with him and everyone could see it but Mark and me. After two months of marriage, I wanted out. I didn't want to be married. This poor guy never knew what hit him. I asked him to leave and told him I didn't want to be married anymore. He was confused but mostly hurt. He had given up everything to move up to Seattle and start a life with me and he trusted that I loved him. He did move back to Colorado and proceeded to send heated letters after I filed for divorce, and of course, I was insulted. He had no right to treat me that way. I, again, was the victim. To make things worse, I needed to maintain my pride with my family and friends so I told them I'd been abused, physically and emotionally. He had never laid a hand on me. He loved me with all his heart and I didn't care. I wanted my freedom back. After I sobered up and started making amends, I was able to find him via the internet. I wrote him a letter and he was very surprised to hear from me and I was surprised he was so gracious in accepting my apology. I would have expected (and deserved) a few choice words of admonishment.

TRUST OF EMPLOYERS

My employers trusted me to do my job. Because of late nights I called in sick a lot or worse, I would show up for work barely sober. I was able to function during my government career; however, I let my "drinking do the thinking", and left after fifteen years because the traveling kept me away from my favorite bar. One of my drinking companions owned a construction company and offered me a job as an office manager and assistant project manager trainee. Since he and I had basically the same priorities (booze), it was a match made in heaven.

My ability to function diminished by the time I started working for a school district in Southern California. My attendance was sporadic at best and my performance started to suffer. By the time I entered rehab, I was on the verge of disciplinary action. I was president of the local school employee union and I created quite a reputation with the board members and the district superintendent. When issues arose regarding an employee or a contract matter I would pick up the phone, no matter how late, and call one of them and give them my drunken opinion. This continued throughout my presidency and they all lost a great deal of sleep. I was fortunate they were sympathetic and supportive in my sobriety endeavor. They welcomed me back from rehabilitation leave with open arms. In fact, the superintendent told me when I came back, with a smile on his face, that my sobriety not only saved me, but gave him the opportunity to catch up on his sleep!

I would like to say my performance and attendance improved after my return; however, it did not. Working on my sobriety, plus a failing marriage created a chaotic atmosphere and it was difficult for me to focus and keep my personal life separate from the job. I ended up leaving because I was not dependable and I knew that eventually they would have let me go. At least sobriety brought me to accepting reality. I didn't point fingers at someone else for this failure; I actually took responsibility and did the right thing.

TRUST OF CO-WORKERS

My co-workers also suffered considerably. I used them horrifically to obtain goals in my career, lifestyle and relationships. I was the worst of the worst. I leeched on to them until I sucked them dry. I would take credit for their work, blame them for errors and expect them to cover me when I came in late, left early or came in barely sober. Whenever confronted I was an expert at twisting things around so I would end up looking like the victim. There were a few occasions when I wasn't successful, but even then, I justified my actions to myself and went on my merry way looking for more people to take advantage of.

One case in particular was right before I hit my bottom. I was working at an elementary school and one of the women there always rubbed me the wrong way. *Carol was very independent, intelligent and productive. She knew what needed to get done and did it. She was respected by management a great deal and I was extremely jealous. We had to work together closely and from all outward appearances, we got along. I was nice to her while she was around but would constantly talk behind her back, joke about her appearance and mannerisms and try to find some way to make her fail or at least look less perfect. One day she came up to me and told me she was aware of what I was doing and didn't appreciate it. Her approach was gentle and kind, but of course, I lied and said she was way out of line and didn't know what she was talking about. She looked at me with very sad (and pitying) eyes and walked away. For some reason, I felt shame and guilt, which was not the norm, but as I said, I was getting close to my bottom. Carol, being the classy woman she was, did not report it to our administrator, she let it go. Once I got sober, I planned on making amends to her; however, I kept putting it off. She passed away not too long ago, after a brief illness, so I never got the chance to tell her how much I had admired her and how sorry I was that I treated her so poorly.

TRUST OF GOD

The biggest theft of trust was the trust given to me by God. I'll address my abortions later; however, God entrusted me with two babies and I aborted them. The babies in my womb trusted me as well. They were safe inside of me and had a future ahead of them and I took it all away. God also entrusted me with a body to bear more children and I violated that trust by having a tubal ligation. I ignored His will for me and lost the opportunity to experience the miracle of birth. God entrusted me with a wonderful family and many friends and I took advantage of that. I wreaked havoc on them all, used them for my own desires and goals. He entrusted me with common sense and morals and I threw them all away as well. All that trust He gave me was a gift. I took that gift and abused it.

I learned the journey to forgiveness is a long and arduous road. The only way I could rebuild and earn the trust of family, friends, employers and co-workers was to walk the walk and talk the talk. I now try my hardest to think through my actions before taking them and when in a difficult situation, hold my tongue until the right (and honest) words come. Humility is something I've always struggled with but I know when I do violate a trust, humbling myself by accepting responsibility and asking for forgiveness is imperative to my spiritual and emotional growth. Realizing I caused so much hurt and violated so much trust has made me more willing to change. God is patient, kind and loving – and wants us to be like Him. I'm not perfect, but with His help and wisdom, I'm on the right path.

Chapter 8
Lies, Lies and More Lies

"No man who practices deceit shall dwell in my house;
no man who utters lies shall continue in my presence".

Psalms 101:7

To quote House, M.D., "Everybody lies". That is the truth and there's no disputing it. Most people tell little white lies instead of hurting someone's feelings, or to avoid getting into confrontations, while some lie to get out of trouble or get ahead. I lied out of habit. I didn't have to have a reason, I just did it. I got so wound up in those webs of deceit I couldn't find my way out.

During an affair with a married co-worker, I wanted to see what he would do if I told him I was pregnant. I went over to his desk with tears in my eyes and asked him if he would meet me in the mail room. Through sobs I blurted it out and waited for his reaction. I was secretly hoping he would throw his arms around me and tell me how much he loved me and that he would leave his wife (then I would fake a miscarriage), but that didn't happen. Nothing happened. He didn't show any emotion whatsoever. He just looked at me and told me he would pay for an abortion. I gave him the price and he gave me the money. He never asked me about the procedure and if he had I would have fabricated a complete scenario on the pain, agony, etc., that I had gone through. We continued our fling and the pregnancy and subsequent abortion was never discussed. I justified keeping the money because he "owed me". Prostitution?

One lie I lived for over thirty years. Although I've confessed to family and some friends about it, there are still people out there that think I'm the most wonderful person in the world for my great sacrifice, and for that I'm sorry.

Back around 1978, I became friends with a gal that worked in my building. We would go out for drinks after work and talk for hours. One night she told me a secret she had been holding on to. She had been pregnant and given up her baby for adoption. Well, being drunk and trying to be compassionate and understanding, I told her, "Wow! That's a coincidence, I did too!" We talked for hours and hours about our experiences and we became best friends. I told her I had gotten pregnant by a guy in the Navy but I didn't want to marry him. I decided to keep the baby but was unable to because of finances so I let him take her. He got married to someone else and I let her adopt "Jennifer". I continued by telling her that after a few years I decided it was best to cut contact because it wasn't fair to Jennifer's mom. Boy could I weave a tale. Well, that became my "drunken story". Whenever someone new came into my life, I would share that secret. I would tell them I'd never told anyone before, and ask that it not be repeated. I wanted everyone to know what a selfless thing I did by placing my child in a better environment but I didn't want them to tell anyone else (I didn't want to get caught in a lie). I was so convincing, my sister even believed me. I had called her one night in a drunken stupor and I made her promise she would never tell my folks. I even had pictures. They were pictures of an old boyfriend's daughter. At one point I decided I needed more attention so I created a whole new scenario that Jennifer ran away from her home to find me, got involved with drugs and died from an overdose. Boy was that good for a few "feel sorry for Patti" months. After that I wanted to just drop the whole adoption story but I couldn't stop myself. I still needed people to think I was someone special.

Although those lies were bad enough, I had several others – too many to count - in my repertoire of attention grabbers. I recall being out with a group of co-workers one night and decided it was time for some drama. I broken down in tears and told them I was going blind and had only a few years of eyesight left. These poor people were so compassionate and caring, it breaks my heart to this day. I also claimed to be married to a New England Patriot (living in Seattle?), tutoring Dustin Hoffman (in what?) and having parents that were millionaires. In my mind, I thought the "real" Patti was not good enough.

The worst lies of all were those I told myself. I firmly believed my actions were justified. Looking back, there was guilt involved in everything I did but I had repressed it all and replaced it with pride, anger, lust and vengeance. I was a wretched failure and convinced myself I was wonderful. I took absolutely no responsibility for anything. I was always the victim and whoever I hurt definitely deserved it. I convinced myself I was a good decent person that just happened to have drama wherever I went. I never believed in Satan but if I would have honestly looked into the mirror, I think that's who I would have seen.

Author Tad Williams once said, "We tell lies when we are afraid … afraid of what we don't know, afraid of what others will think, afraid of what will be found out about us. But every time we tell a lie, the thing that we fear grows stronger". That is so very true. In a perfect world no one would lie; however, it's not a perfect world.

There's no easy remedy to this situation. Lying is sadly a part of human nature. I know that "honesty is the best policy"; however, it's also sometimes very hard. The best advice I can give is to step back and consider the consequences before saying anything. It's hard and takes a great deal of determination. It's still so much easier for me to blurt out whatever comes to mind but I do my best to think things through. When I'm successful there's a peace that envelopes me. When I'm not, I make every attempt to come clean, make amends and address the lies in the confessional.

Holding myself accountable to my priest is something that has helped me most of all. In the Catholic faith, we believe our priests are "in persona Christi", in other words, in the person of Christ. Although He knows when I lie, He wants me to confess and repent. When I enter that confessional, I am entering a room with Christ, humbling myself by confessing my sins and asking for mercy. It's a cleansing experience to vocalize the lies told (and other sins as well), and a wonderful way to curb temptation and when I look in a mirror today, I can honestly say it's me and not Satan.

Chapter 9

The Innocents

"I call heaven and earth to witness against you this day,
that I have set before you life and death, blessing and curse;
therefore choose life, that you and your descendants may live".
Deuteronomy 30:19

My irresponsible lifestyle resulted in three pregnancies. The first pregnancy was when I was nineteen and I miscarried. There was no mourning, I was actually happy and relieved I wouldn't have to disclose the pregnancy to my parents. The father was also very relieved because back in those days you almost always "had to get married" and who would want to marry me? Regardless, there was no love in that relationship, we were just dating and he was my first sexual encounter. I actually believed him when he said, "You can't get pregnant the first time". He was going to step up to the plate and marry me though, which was quite admirable. Rest in peace Richard Martel.

My second pregnancy was when I was twenty-three, a result of rampant promiscuity. I had a choice at that time of two fathers so I didn't mention it to either one. My career was blossoming in the government and I knew a child would hold me back. The only person that knew was my roommate, Ann, my friend whose husband killed her daughter. Being totally insensitive, I asked her to take me to the abortion. I'm sure that was a turning point in our friendship, me voluntarily killing my child. She didn't say a thing though, and supported me through the whole process. I don't remember everything clearly, but I recall I was not counseled or advised of any residual emotional effects. I remember the sterile atmosphere absent of emotion or caring. I can still hear the vacuum, feel the tugging and the emptiness I experienced after it was over. The relief of no longer being pregnant was there; however, I wasn't the same person anymore. I pushed it all back into my mind and went on with my life. Rest in peace Sarah Catherine.

My third pregnancy was when I was twenty-seven. I did know who the father was; he was barely twenty-one. He was also the brother of that friend and co-worker that had the boyfriend I slept with. This time I decided to keep the baby, but not tell the father. I had a good job with a high salary, and would be able to raise the child on my own. I told everyone at work and all of my friends. I called my parents hoping they would be thrilled, but no surprise, they were quite upset. My mom actually asked me if I knew who the father was (of course I was highly insulted). She had every right to ask, she knew my reputation. She told me I shouldn't raise a child on my own, I had a career to think of and that she and my dad thought it would be best to get an abortion. Well, I hung up on her and unplugged the phone so she couldn't call me back. I started to cry uncontrollably. Being the true self-pitying, self-absorbed alcoholic, I thought my mom told me I would be a terrible mother and they wouldn't be there for me. Instead of going through with the pregnancy I followed through with their advice and had the abortion. When I went in for the procedure, it again was sterile, null of emotion or caring. I heard the same vacuum, felt the tugging and emptiness afterward. The emptiness though was much more devastating. I truly felt something was missing. Again, I pushed it into the dark recesses of my mind. I needed to take time off work for the procedure so instead of being honest, I decided to tell everyone I miscarried. Looking back, I think by telling them that, I wanted some sort of sympathy to assuage my guilt. Rest in peace, Matthew Thomas.

It wasn't until I had sobered up and joined the Catholic Church that the true affects of the abortions were realized. I attended a Faith in the Spirit Seminar at my parish. There was no reason I would go to something like that, but on a weekend I walked into the seminar alone. One of the speakers was talking about her abortion and how it had such an impact on her emotionally. She spoke about Rachel's Hope which does healing retreats for post-abortive women. The more she spoke, the more my tears flowed. She was talking directly to me! After the session, I walked up to Rosemary Benefield, Executive Director of Rachel's Hope, who was also at the seminar and said, "I need you". She gave me a pamphlet that outlined her program and I signed up for her weekend retreat.

I always thought I was a pretty tough cookie, but I did nothing but cry throughout the whole program. The walls I had put up tumbled down and I realized the abortions not only saddled me with mountains of guilt and self-loathing, they catapulted me deeper into my alcoholism and promiscuity. Not only had I self-destructed, at the age of 30, I convinced a doctor to perform a tubal ligation. At the time, I told myself I didn't want to have kids and it would be the best way to avoid any more pregnancies. I know now I was actually punishing myself for what I had done. I didn't deserve to be a mother so I made sure I wouldn't be.

This retreat not only opened up my eyes to the past, it gave me hope for the future. I was already going in the right direction but there was always something that was holding me back. That something definitely was the abortions. I had never mourned my children, even the one I miscarried. I never acknowledged their existence in my womb. I had never confessed my abortions to my priest because when I was baptized in 2006, all my prior sins were washed away; however, the guilt was still there. I didn't feel renewed or cleansed. I had never truly vocalized my abortions or anything of my past so I think in some ways I just thought that was the way it was supposed to be. Not only did the abortions stop my emotional and spiritual grown, my whole ugly past did as well. It all went hand in hand. Rachel's Hope provided me with the emotional and spiritual tools to forgive myself and to connect with my babies. Asking Matthew and Sarah's forgiveness for aborting them was the hardest thing I had ever done but also the most healing. I was told that they were in Heaven rejoicing because their mommy finally acknowledged their existence and I believe that. I also believe they have forgiven me. Confessing the abortions to a priest was also heart-wrenching but when I received absolution, I felt it. God forgave me as well. Matthew and Sarah were dedicated and by the time the retreat was over I had cried a million tears. I was emotionally and physically exhausted but I felt renewed at the same time. I also dedicated Richard Martel, the son I miscarried at a second retreat that I was asked to co-lead. I regretfully failed to acknowledge him during my first retreat because I didn't think it was appropriate to do so. Now the circle was complete and I was at peace. I still mourn and I sometimes fall back into the guilt but I have the ability to work through it, praise God.

"Rachel is weeping for her children. She refuses to be comforted for her children are no more. Thus says the Lord: Wipe the tears from your eyes. The sorrow you have shown shall have its reward." (Jeremiah 31:15-17). This passage is the focus of Rachel's Hope and other organizations that provide post-abortive healing retreats. I had never connected my abortions to any psychological issues prior to attending Rachel's Hope, but during that time, it became crystal clear. After co-leading four retreats (one in a correctional facility), I saw the same unrelenting shame, remorse and self-hatred that I had, but I also witnessed the miraculous transformation. These women, like me, left the retreat with a renewed spirit, a feeling of hope and a true understanding of God's mercy.

Chapter 10

Final Descent

"You will seek me and find me;
when you seek me with all your heart".
Jeremiah 29:13

The morning of November 7, 1997, I called in sick to work, which was not unusual, and started in on a six-pack of beer. I had gotten into the habit of calling in if there was beer still in the fridge after the night before. If there wasn't beer, NyQuil or vanilla sufficed. The more I drank, the deeper I sank into despair. The whole world fell down around me. I realized I was in a loveless marriage, I was a failure as a wife, mother and daughter, and I was alone. I felt empty inside, and hopeless. The emotional pain was excruciating and I wanted it gone. I wanted to die. I went into the bathroom and got a bottle of anti-depressants. I opened it and placed it in front of me on the table. Then, for some reason, instead of putting the pills in my mouth, I picked up the phone and called Alcoholics Anonymous. This was my first experience with Divine intervention, although back then I had no clue.

Through AA's hotline, contacts were made and I was taken to a psychiatric hospital. The admissions process was very demoralizing. I knew I needed help, but I couldn't understand why they were so intrusive. They searched my suitcase, purse, and clothing for anything that could cause bodily harm or contained alcohol. They confiscated my shoelaces, toothbrush and comb. I was evaluated although I felt more like I was being judged. I couldn't answer half the questions, and the ones I did, I don't think I made any sense. During the evaluation I admitted I wanted to end my life and when asked if I might have a drinking problem I said yes. I finally told the truth.

I don't know what they gave me but I slept a lot and when I was awake, I did nothing but cry. I know now the medication was to help me with the detoxification process and get me back to some level of sanity. Once the alcohol was out of my system and I had gone through withdrawal, they deemed me no longer a danger to myself. They explained to me my suicidal tendencies were due to depression brought on by my abuse of alcohol. I was transferred to the rehab ward, my belongings were returned to me and I was formally introduced to Alcoholics Anonymous (AA).

Once released from the hospital, I entered outpatient rehab and started going to AA meetings. I was on leave from my job so I had a great deal of time to concentrate on sobriety. I immersed myself in rehab and meetings, got a sponsor and started working the twelve steps. Jim (my second husband) wasn't really happy with what was going on and did not want to participate in the family portion of my outpatient program. He reluctantly went a few times but stopped because he felt it was a waste of time. My son and step-sons went a couple of times as well but they could have cared less. I had also asked Jim to go to Al-Anon secretly hoping he would realize he too had a problem. He did go to a few meetings and that was it. He told our son years later the only reason he went to a few meetings was to find out what was wrong with me. He continued to drink and didn't hide the booze which made my staying sober very hard; however, my sponsor, Dottie B., was aware of the situation and kept me busy and away from the house as much as possible. In fact, at my very first meeting she walked up, gave me her address and told me I WILL pick her up for the noon meeting every day. She scared the heck out of me so I did pick her up and followed all of her directions for fear of repercussions. She was what they called an "Oldtimer" and did the tough love type of sponsoring. She didn't pull any punches, wouldn't let me make excuses and dragged me along, sometimes kicking and screaming...but it worked. Along with Dottie B., my parents and boss were my biggest cheerleaders, which was unbelievable. I didn't deserve their help or support at all. I guess they hoped that sobriety would allow me to finally climb out of the hole I'd been in and become the type of person I was capable of being.

I was desperate to heal and for once in my miserable life, listened to guidance and actually followed through. Doing the personal inventory was very difficult and at the time I did my best; however, there were many demons still hidden deep within my soul. I made amends when I could and got very involved in the program, taking meeting commitments like making coffee or being a secretary. I was told not to make any drastic changes in the first year so I didn't, but after that year I did separate from Jim and filed for divorce. I was on my own again but this time it was different ... I was different.

Chapter 11
Conversion

*"Therefore, if any one is in Christ, he is a new creation;
the old has passed away, behold, the new has come."*
2 Corinthians 5:17

My current husband, Mike, is a cradle-Catholic but was not
practicing his faith when we got together and I had never been
baptized. I was supposed to get baptized Methodist; however, it
never happened due to that baseball accident. His brother and sister-
in-law, who are practicing Catholics, invited us to go to church with
them. We continued to attend and one day I called my sister-in-law
and asked her how to become Catholic. I so much loved the services
and I realized I needed God and a faith community in my life. AA
had given me a higher power but I wanted more. She, of course, was
thrilled and admitted to me she had prayed that I would ask her. I
signed up for RCIA (Rite of Christian Initiation for Adults) and
started the classes. I learned a lot about the faith and fell more and
more in love with God. During that time, Mike came into full
communion with the church. We also wanted to have our marriage
blessed so went through the annulment processes, counseled with
our priest and had a beautiful ceremony with family and friends.
After the ceremony we felt renewed. It was like we were newlyweds
all over again and our love was stronger than ever.

During RCIA preparation for Easter Vigil, I was told that once I
entered the water of baptism all my prior sins would be forgiven. I
was relieved, thinking I would not have to actually tell anyone I had
such a wretched and evil past. I have to admit, when I did enter the
baptismal font I secretly thought the water would start boiling as I
had too much sin for it to handle. Thankfully that didn't happen, but
nothing else did either. I didn't feel cleansed and I didn't feel that

close to God. I attended Mass and started participating in a variety of activities within the parish hoping that would bring me closer to Him, but there was something that was holding me back.

I was going through a really rough period with my son and having a great deal of spiritual problems. No matter how many Masses I attended, rosaries prayed, books read, I was regressing in my faith journey. After many years of sobriety I even considered starting to drink again. That dark abyss that God pulled me out of was pulling me back and I didn't know how to stop it.

I return to that Faith in the Spirit Seminar which guided me to Rachel's Hope. During that retreat, if you recall, I confessed my abortions to a priest. I did feel forgiveness and absolution for the abortions and realized maybe my other past sins needed to be addressed as well. Prior to the retreat I had been participating in reconciliation services twice a year at my parish but limited my confessions to those sins committed after my baptism.

A General Confession is a private confession where you confess all past sins and that's exactly what I needed; however, the thought of going through all of my past, face-to-face with a priest was very horrifying. We had a new priest and I knew he was going to be aghast at having such a wanton woman in his parish and would want me to leave. Well, obviously that didn't happen. Father Fernando was compassionate, kind, understanding and accepting. I'm surprised he could understand me as I was sobbing throughout the whole thing. I was crying for my son, my unborn children, the hurt I caused everyone and for who I had been. That watershed moment was like another baptism for me, but this baptism left me cleansed and absolved, and thanks to Father Fernando, closer to God than I had ever been.

Chapter 12
I Am What I Am

"But by the grace of God I am what I am, and his grace toward me was not in vain. On the contrary, I worked harder than any of them, though it was not I, but the grace of God which is with me."
1 Corinthians 15:10

I'm far from perfect and continue to make mistakes but it is different now. I am aware of how my actions or inactions affect me spiritually, emotionally and physically and how they affect my family, friends and community. I have learned to open my heart to God and ask for guidance. I know that no matter how bad things get God is with me. During those demon days I had put myself in very dangerous situations; picking up total strangers in bars, driving drunk and wanting to end my life. He kept reaching out His hand to me and even though I refused, He persisted until I grabbed it. My demise was not part of His master plan. He has much more in store for me and I am filled with joyful anticipation.

Today I have a very full life. It's not free from ups and downs and healing from my past is a work in progress. Staying sober will always be a challenge; however, working the Twelve Steps of Alcoholics Anonymous, and the support of family and friends gives me the strength to persevere one day at a time. I have sixteen years of sobriety which is an absolute miracle. I now have a solid marriage based on faith, love and respect. Michael and I are active participants in our parish and look forward to becoming more involved once he retires.

I recently retired from my career as background investigator to care for my parents and uncle and am using my spare time to focus on writing Christian devotionals. I co-lead Rachel's Hope retreats which gives me the opportunity to reach out to other women who desperately need healing, including those incarcerated. I see hope in the eyes of these women and witnessing their healing magnifies my belief in the never ending love and mercy of God.

I have journeyed from the darkness to the light and am amazed each and every day that I survived. God was always there and I know that no matter what, God loves me and He loves you too. Reach up and let Him grasp your hand.

Acknowledgements

As stated earlier, writing about my failings was a humbling experience. Recalling my actions and the consequences brought a realization that I truly have been blessed. Not only did I survive, I was divinely guided on a path that brought wonderful people into my life. Praise God!

My loving husband, Michael, has the patience of Job. Not only did he give me the time and personal space to write, he encouraged me to continue through my periods of shame and fear. I garnered the courage to let him read the draft, waiting for him to turn away but he held me and continued loving me.

My parents deserved so much more than they received and despite all the pain I inflicted on them, they still love me. When anyone speaks of unconditional love my first thoughts are of them.

My son is a great source of pride. I cannot take any credit for who he is today. He worked through his atrocious childhood with a determination I will never be able to comprehend. We might have our share of disagreements, but I love him for who he is and for blessing me with two beautiful granddaughters.

Dottie B. - my first AA sponsor and loving friend who showed me how to love and appreciate a life of sobriety. She's now with God but she'll always be in my heart.

Last, but most definitely not least … My spiritual heroes: Father Fernando Ramirez, Rob and Nancy Gruning, Rosemary Benefield and Leslie Brunolli. They listened, they counseled and never once passed judgment. My continued healing is a direct result of their support and compassion.

Appendix

The following article was written by Jim Benefield, LMFT, who graciously permitted me to use to summarize my story.

Turning Your Lifelong Regrets into Immeasurable Graces
Cedars of Lebanon, Newsletter of the John Paul II Institute of
Christian Spirituality
June 2001

Nowadays, courses on "Human Development" teach that we have the ability to remember past experiences in minute detail. We now know that our ability to store memories begins during the first nine months of life. In his book *Babies Remember Birth*, David Chamberlain, PhD., shows that newborns remember the events of their gestation, and that it is even possible for adults to recall the events surrounding their gestation and birth. Whenever memories of experiences like these are stimulated, a flood of feelings can be released. Many of these memories and associated feelings are painful. The memory of painful experiences, in turn, often lead to regret – a feeling of permanent loss occasioned by the memory of some painful event.

Without the miraculous gift of bi-location, that God gives to saints like Padre Pio or Venerable Mary of Agreda, we cannot be in two places at the same time. Nor can we be "at two times in the same space." In our ordinary human condition, we move forward in time in a linear and progressive way. Consequently, we cannot recreate one second in time nor erase a single unpleasant experience. We own each past moment of our lives, whether we like it or not – whether those past moments were shaped by our own actions or by the actions of others. We have no more control over the past than we have over the color of our skin, the identify of our parents, the affluence of our families, or what happened to us during most of our early years.

The Regions of Regret

Some have said, "I was in the wrong place at the wrong time", or, "I wish that I was born at a different time", but the bare fact remains. What has been done cannot be physically undone. Once an act is realized, that act remains a part of real-time history, never to be erased. In the progressive momentum of time, one's circumstances may change for the better or worse according to one's opportunities. And even though some original acts that can be rectified by succeeding opportunities, other regrettable acts leave a lasting legacy of shame, self-hatred, anger and depression.

These are the regions of regret. "If only I had a second chance", "I wish I could take everything back that I said", "I'm so sorry that I had the abortion; hit my wife; sexually abused my child; have to go to jail because I burglarized a car; ever used drugs; punched my mom; received a sexually transmitted disease because of promiscuous sex at such an early age." Often times the consequences of an act can follow throughout one's life without relief from emotional pain because one cannot undo what has been done within the limits of linear time and physical distance.

When people lose their ability to focus on the present with hope for the future because of the traumas and failures of the past, they easily become prey to depression and despair. In their self-absorption, hopeless people cannot see God and what He might be doing through the events that they regret. Their anger and even hatred towards others hold them back from looking into the merciful eyes of God.

Thankfully, Jesus is not bound by linear time or physical distance: "Jesus is the same yesterday, today and forever." By his divine-human power, Jesus has borne all of our sorrows. By his divine-human power, Jesus has perfectly atoned for each and every one of our sins. Moreover, Jesus has prepared a perfect life for each of us. As St. Paul wrote in his letter to the Ephesians, "We are God's handiwork, **created in Christ Jesus for good works that He has prepared for us beforehand that we should walk in them**" (Ephesians 2:10). Jesus has gone before us to offer the Father all of our sins, washed in his Precious Blood. For this present moment, and for each future present moment of our lives, Jesus has prepared a perfect act of love for us to do together with Him, for the glory of the Father, and for the good of all souls, past, present, and future. Making friends with past losses and regrets by purposefully giving them back to God with Jesus and placing them in his providential hand opens the way to total freedom from the bondage of living in regrets.

A Spiritual Exercise to Attain Freedom from Past Regrets

In the course of my practice, I have discovered a spiritual exercise that can help to bring about this liberation from past regrets. In this article, I will describe this exercise as a testimony to the infinite mercy of Jesus Christ whose redeeming love embraces the past, the present, and the future. If you wish to perform this exercise, you will need to set several hours aside to do so slowly and prayerfully. If you prefer simply to read the exercise, you may; however, all of us, if we search deeply, will find multiple regrets: wishing that we had done this or not done that, sorrowful over what we should have done or didn't do. Freedom from regret can be achieved by submitting one's entire past to the Precious Blood of Jesus. This exercise is not the only way to do so, but it is an effective way.

Face Your Regrets

The first step to freedom from past regrets is to describe them in detail. Explain what you regret having lost in terms of past, present, and future opportunities. For example, "My life would have been so much better if I had not been adopted into this dysfunctional family," or "If I had worked harder at my grades, I would have been able to go to the school of my choice." Express your anger at yourself and at others. When you have finished expressing your anger, imagine yourself wrapping your regrets into "a package". Then visualize yourself going into the Garden of Gethsemane and presenting your package of regrets to Jesus in his agony.

As you present this package of regrets to Jesus, He invites you to kneel down with Him and you hear Him say, "I will make something good of this." And then you see Jesus do a very strange thing: He takes your package of regrets, and as he places them together with the multitude of regrets already before him in the garden, He pulls you close to Himself and begins to sob uncontrollably. As He sobs, you hear Him pray to His Heavenly Father. He sees that these regrets have seriously impeded a healthy trustful relationship between you and your Heavenly Father. His prayer to his Father is filled with compassion on your behalf.

You lean close to hear Him pray: "My dear Father, I know that you will refuse Me nothing. I bring you this child whose heartaches and disappointments have interfered with his ability to love and trust You. Father, he is your child, and I ask that You not hold this against him. He has been blinded by so much sorrow that all he sees is himself and his regrets. He doesn't see Us and our love for him. Heal the anger in his soul, and by your grace do not let him be dominated by self-loathing, resentments, hostility and unforgiveness towards himself and others.

"Oh merciful and forgiving Father, touch him with the fire of your forgiveness and plunge this fire into the deepest recesses of his being, so that he is moved also to seek out forgiveness from You for those that have harmed him. Remove this bondage of hate and let him no longer be ruled by it. Remove the dismal outlook that he has for his future and fill him with hope and knowledge of Our love for him. Give him all that he needs so that he can receive forgiveness for himself and hold on to Your forgiveness as his most precious gift from You.

"By the power that I have in You, I hereby declare this soul free from the destructive effects of the regrets of his past that he has not been able to let go. I declare him free from the harm that he has done to himself and others, and from the harm that others have done to him. Let healing flow into those who have been wounded by his actions and omissions, and when the time is right let there be reconciliation between them.

"Place your hands over his heart and seal it with a confident faith in your provincial care for him. Let him see the regrets that he has clung to so tenaciously as "your branding mark" that will forever bind him to your love for all to see. As surely as the cattleman brands his steer for all to know its ownership, so let it be with him. Even as You have used my wounds of the crucifixion to draw mankind back to You, so let his wounds be joined with Mine, co-mingled with my suffering for the expiation of sin and the conversion of souls. Even as none of my suffering was wasted, do not let one morsel of his suffering go unused for your divine purpose."

As Jesus prays, you notice that your package of anger and regrets is saturated with his tears and by droplets of the blood from the "sweat" of his brow. Jesus holds on to you even more tightly and concludes, "I thank you for receiving and honoring this prayer on "John's behalf" even as you receive and honor me."

The Challenge of the Cross

And now, Jesus looks at you, his eyes burning with love. Those compassionate eyes plead with you to accept forgiveness from the Heavenly Father. And, as the fire of his love penetrates your very soul, you become aware of an eternal request that only you can answer. "Will you accept your regrets as a cross that only you can carry – for the expiation of sin and for the conversion of souls – so that by your intention you can join with Me to help make reparation to the Father and to love Him on behalf of all?"

At this moment you have a choice: "Will you choose to resent these painful experiences, which means fighting against grace and mercy and staying in guilt, grief and despair? Or, will you choose to live with these regret, which may represent sadness and permanent losses, as your gift to the Trinitarian lover, with the intention of standing in prayer for many?"

Through the example of heroic men and women in the scriptures and throughout history, you know that many have been blessed and saved because of the actions of the few. You instinctively know what your choice at this moment is critical. You hear yourself saying, "I will let this be my cross, and I am resolved to pick up my cross daily and follow you as your disciple. **(Let yourself feel the relief that comes with making that choice in faith, and let the power of the Trinitarian Godhead rush through you!)**

Now Jesus wants to invite you to join with Him in prayer as He prays for so many who are being held in bondage by their inability to let go of their painful past. You hear yourself say, "I thank you for all this forgiveness that You pour out upon me and upon all souls as freely as torrential waters that fall from the sky and soak the earth. I humbly receive all that You have for me." And then the strangest sentences come out of your mouth: "This is too much of a gift for me to keep to myself. I implore you, Lord, to let me go with You into every heart that is in need of your forgiveness so that I can speak to them of your abundant love. Let me plead to the Father with You on behalf of all those who need to forgive others and who need to let go of their painful regrets. Let us go quickly so that souls can be reconciled with You and avoid falling deeper into the depths of despair."

To your surprise, you find yourself filled with compassion for souls who have been in your situation, and in that compassion you feel an urgency to pray for them. You turn to Jesus who is suffering so much over these regrets because they represent a multitude of souls of the whole human family. It seems as if time has stood still as you see Jesus take each bundle of regrets and clutch them to Himself while interceding on each one's behalf. You see that there are many souls who cannot accept his love and mercy, who will choose to stay in their unforgiveness, regret and despair. And you see that this causes Jesus infinitely more pain and makes Him sweat even more blood.

Throughout your Christian Life, you have asked Jesus to compassionate you for what you have gone through. Now, you find yourself compassionating Jesus for what He has suffered on your behalf. Only love could do this. In your compassion for Jesus, you express your sincere sorrow for ever having doubted Him. You want to apologize to Jesus on behalf of the whole human family, from the first man to the last, for all the times we have not trusted in Him to help us in our moments of crisis. (It was in those times that we trusted more in ourselves and in others. Oh Jesus, forgive our foolishness!) As you continue to compassionate Jesus in all that He suffers, you notice that He is looking somewhat more refreshed. His glance tells you that He is most pleased to have found someone who is willing to spend time consoling Him as He suffers – as He makes reparation to the Father for all the wrongs that have been committed against Him – someone who will also make reparation to the Heavenly Father for offenses committed against Him. Your words to Jesus as you prepare yourself to leave are filled with gratitude for having freed you from the bondage of regrets.

The Principle of Forgiveness

The principle of forgiveness is cyclical: God wants to forgive, and his infinite mercy flows to us through his son Jesus. Indeed, He wants us to desire His forgiveness. But to desire is not enough. He wants us to accept His love and forgiveness and to forgive all those who have harmed us. But even this is not enough. He also wants us to compassionate Jesus in the sufferings He endured on our behalf so that we will be set free from self-centeredness. Then He wants us to go and spread the message of forgiveness wherever we can. And finally, to complete the cyclical process, He wants us to come before Jesus and then to Him for his merciful love and forgiveness, for ourselves and for the whole human family.

In my experience, it is gratitude to the Trinity that insures permanent healing. Without continuous gratitude, chances are that the doors of depression and despair will reopen. On the other hand, when one shoulders his burden of past sins and traumas – in union with the sufferings of Christ for the salvation of souls – the Holy Trinity turns the natural consequences of those regrettable acts into a supernatural source of grace. Through our union with the divine-human life of Jesus, this grace benefits not only the one making the sacrifice, but all souls – past, present and future.

Made in the USA
San Bernardino, CA
20 March 2015